CW00539228

By the author

Staring Directly at the Eclipse

Travelling Second Class Through Hope

Raining Upwards

Art By Johnny ★

A Normal Family ✦

This Phantom Breath

The Department of Lost Wishes

Swallowing the Entire Ocean

Strikingly Invisible

The Escape Plan

★ Collated and edited by Henry Normal

✦ With Angela Pell and published by Two Roads

The Escape Plan

HENRY NORMAL
THE ESCAPE PLAN

Flapjack Press
www.flapjackpress.co.uk

Exploring the synergy between performance and the page

Published in 2020 by Flapjack Press
Salford, Gtr Manchester
⊕ flapjackpress.co.uk

ISBN 978-1-9161479-4-2

Cover art by Johnny Carroll-Pell
f Art By Johnny
⊙ johnnycarrollpell
Photographs courtesy of the author

Cover design by Paul Neads
⊕ paulneads.co.uk

Printed by Imprint Digital
Upton Pyne, Exeter, Devon
⊕ imprintdigital.com

FSC

MAN
CHE
STER
City of
Literature

*I would like to thank Angela Pell, Linda Hallam,
Penny Shepherd, Theresa Sowerby, Colette Bryce,
Matt Welton, Ross Bradshaw and Paul Neads
for their help in bringing this collection together.*

This book is dedicated to ...

Anyone whose name is such
that it will boost my fame
lend me some much needed literary credibility
and help shift more units

Anyone in a position
to do me a favour in the future
(who is easily impressed
by token gestures)

Anyone I feel duty bound to acknowledge
as I know them really well and I've not
dedicated a book to them yet

Anyone who I know vaguely but I want
to exaggerate the closeness of my relationship with
in a formal semi-permanent
cost-effective fashion

Anyone whose name is not easily recognisable
as it's just a name I made up to pretend
I know someone well enough
to dedicate a book to them

Anyone at random
like a fishing expedition
for a new friend

In fact, anyone I've not dedicated a book to already
if there is anyone left in that category
still alive on Earth

Yes there is
Me

This book is dedicated to myself
I did all the bloody work
It's about time I got a book dedicated to me
It's no use me waiting round for you to write a book
and dedicate it to me
That's never going to happen

No... I'm joking
This book is dedicated to
You

Yes you holding this book in your hand
wondering whether to purchase it
(if you haven't done already)
To be honest you've shown more interest
in this collection so far than anyone I know
therefore it's dedicated to you

Surely you've got to buy it now
It might be the only work
that's ever dedicated specifically to you

Ask if you can get discount

Contents

I. *Staring Directly at the Eclipse*

The breath within the balloon — 19
If signatures reflect personality they cannot all remain ... — 20
I am not belittled by your culture of ambition — 21
There is love at first sight — 22
The house is not the same since you left — 23
The missing page — 24
The last parents — 25
A prayer for the rejected — 26
Skin — 27
Photos with my son — 28
The frame of the Mona Lisa dreams — 29
Logic is not a feeling — 30
Summer on Pluto — 31
Abiogenesis to revelations — 32
The eating of a unicorn — 33
The joy of frogs — 34
King Canute should have checked the tides — 35
Cueva de las Manos — 36
The first spark has led to this blaze — 37
If you should ever climb a tree — 38
A gift — 39
The questions they don't ask on the census — 40
Staring directly at the eclipse — 41
Is memory thought or emotion? — 42
Beauty without numbers — 44
This is not a house of war — 45
The dream ticket — 46
Telegraph poles and ships' masts — 48
Night fishing — 49
Sand between the toes — 50
Tinned fruit and evaporated milk — 51

Photo-bombing God   52
Gravestones at a wedding   54
The ulterior motivator   55
A kind of loving   56
An offering to the people of the mounds   57
The couple next door – a sharing experience   58
The garden is still there underneath   60
Vanguard of audacious   61
Does a bad curtain call ruin a show?   62
A prayer for the hesitant   64

II. *Travelling Second Class Through Hope*

Sans pretension   67
The Dinosaur War poems   68
Never play chess with an anarcho-nihilist   71
Ten ways to end a relationship   72
All kids are born with long thin moustaches   73
No game show will ever hold your worth   74
Mime doesn't pay   75
The lost generation of mermen and mermaids   76
Travelling second class through Hope   77
Plain biscuits   78
A happy ending (revised)   79
Love like Hell   80

III. *Raining Upwards*

With zero the house always wins   83
Who wasn't out to sea didn't pray to God   84
Tunnelling into space   85
As the ground accelerates towards you at an acute angle   86
The Second Punic War is not available on a tea towel   87
A stream of consciousness meets the ocean   88
Pictures of you without me   90
The remnants of a gymkhana   91

"And wilt thou bend a listening ear to praises low as ours"   92
An imaginary fly cannot be captured   93
Twice as many hydrogen atoms as oxygen moving   94
The smell of freshly cut grass is a communication   95
I'd like you to know   96
"And can you, then, who have such possessions ..."   97
You've got me but who's got you?   98
Christmas at the end of the world   99
Fame as a perpetual wedding   100
Exploring rockpools   101
Hominin footprints in Laetoli   102
This season of new life   103
Electric like a tree praising the sky   104
Raining upwards   105
Deafness and social cohesion   106
Horizontal amid horticulture   107
There's more to lemons than being yellow   108
Are other animals afraid of their own species?   109
If you never saw this tree it must be difficult to imagine ...   110
The March of Progress   111
At the hearth of the winter sky   112
Auditioning for the X-men in the Wetlands   113
Windswept and drunk on oxygen   114
Pilgrimage for the agnostic   115
Guadalupe and the navigator   116
The sheet music of Microwave Background Radiation   117
The foghorn has long since given up   118
Eskimo kiss   120
The movement of shadows on the moon   121
Exquisite   122
First prize   123
You won't find a box to tick on any form for this   124
This is merely blossom, fruit will follow   125
Leakage   126
There is a ghost on the shoreline taking a selfie   127

There are layers of cloud moving in different directions   128
The walking wounded at Lidl   129
Reclaimed   130
A little slope of meadow outside my window   131
Near miss   132
Hold me with certainty in this heavenly chaos   134
Pivot   135
Witness   136

IV. *This Phantom Breath*

One autumn noon   139
You lower your eyes   140
Things to do list   142
The clouds surrender dawn   143
A line in the sand   144
Being in love   146
A photo of a sandcastle is a hymn to all loss   147
Where dust makes its home   148
Faith in others   150
Still the root remains   151
Nondescript   152
Wheat field with crows   154
What to say to visitors on Halloween   155
Poetry escapes me   156
Sorry if I'm obscuring your view of God   158
Though we are now in shadow the sun still lights ...   160
An old wedding photo in a garden rich with colour   161
Distance   162
Insult to the brain   164
Jacaranda, a long way from home   165
A '99' in the fog   166
Something wicked this way comes   168
"In thy orisons be all my sins remembered" ...   169
An overdue thank you to microbiotica   170
I'm told that days will start to get longer   172

V. *The Department of Lost Wishes*

The coaster – mighty bastion of civilisation   175
Green poem   176
Is red the colour of passion?   176
Columbus thought the world not in fact round but ...   176
Third World War poems   177
On stepping out the door all past autumns inhaled   178
Sagrada Família (The Sacred Family)   180
The rhapsody of the florist and the butcher   180
Natasia   180
Earlobes   181
In defence of the moustache   182
The genius of Michelangelo   184
Titian a bag   184
A tribute to Andy Warhol's wig   184
Confessions of a closet celibate   185
Chelsea Hotel   186
Lincoln Memorial   186
The trainspotter of love   186
The department of lost wishes   187
Cardigans to the Middle East   188
Waiting for loco   190
Middle-age spread   190
Mid-Wales crisis   190
The poem within you   191
The last poem I ever wrote   192
The measuring of worth   194

VI. *Swallowing the Entire Ocean*

Hello   197
Some people   198
Complication   201
Dry humour – a cautionary verse   202
Brighton nudist beach twinned with Vila do Bispo ...   202

Nature versus synthetic polymers   203
A boy can clap louder than the breakers   204
You can inhale the dead man's fingers from the car park   206
Not unlike the Grand Old Duke of York but without ...   208
I take the twenty-first century into my garden   209
Paranoia   210
Through my car windscreen in the rain I can recreate ...   212
Poem in the shape of an arts grant application   213
Diary for no-one in particular   214
Abusive body language   215
Foreword for a book of poetry I have not actually read   216
I can hear my son enjoying colour   218
Queen Victoria and her Nottingham lace stockings   220
Privates' progress   220
A compendium of woes   221
Sharing a summer sunset   222
Review of the show   224
How are you   226
A rented cremation   227
A close relationship unsung   228
Permanent marker doesn't work on wet sand   231
Quintessence   232
Out of place   234
Twelve raisins at the feast of St Sylvester   235
Thank you   236

VII. *Strikingly Invisible*

20 FAQ about tonight's event (answers)   241
Cuckmere Haven   242
How to make an underclass   243
Philosophical tapas   244
The only flags on the moon are white ...   244
Under a mackerel sky like alien skin   245
Eavesdropping on the gossip of small birds   246
Sitting with Colin Orchard at Stanmer Park   247

To fill two birds with one scone   248
The devil wore Primark   249
Warning – deconstruction in progress   250
MOT for a wedding anniversary   253
Lady with the hood   254
A little slope of meadow (revisited)   255
After Joyce Kilmer   256
Shady lady – Rosa Banksiae   256
Disclaimer   257
Hot under the choleric (an intoler–rant)   258
Looking forward to a mid-life crisis   260
Poolside   261
End game   262
Strikingly invisible   263

The escape plan   265

THE ESCAPE PLAN

I

from

STARING DIRECTLY AT THE ECLIPSE

The breath within the balloon

The breath within the balloon will not last
You never get inflated balloons
on the *Antiques Road Show*
Breath brings with it vulnerability

If never inflated
a balloon may last forever
but such limp reason
will never enchant a child
with decoration
or gladden the heart
with the stretching of possibility
and the fulfilment of promise

Is not a universe of such balloons sadder
than a universe where balloons are apt to burst?

I hold your breath within my hands

The breath within the balloon will not last
but the giving of breath
and the tying of the knot
at each new birth
is an offering
for our choice of worlds

If signatures reflect personality they cannot all remain constant

It's not that I've forgotten my own name
it's just that my signature doesn't flow naturally like it used to

I hesitate as the pen blotches the first ink, self-conscious
Each letter has become foreign, a random code of symbols

With deliberate forgery I have to match up my commitment
with a genuine signature that has already been approved

I'm cribbing off my own past

It's as if my signature is trying to change but is restrained
by the functional need of the authorised version

Strange how we set our own guidelines, our own parameters
so early for something so permanent

I remember practising my signature as a teenager
I'm sure I never understood this was to remain
unchanged forever

As a result my signatures have become clumsy
like a child's crayon letters

I suppose I'm worried if I just sign a new signature
this will not be accepted

Is it possible to authorise a change of signature?
How will I sign for it?

I am not belittled by your culture of ambition

My wife has a moustache
It is plastic
It came out of a Christmas cracker

We are monarchy
in our paper hats

I am King Superman in his favourite cardigan
full of pud

It's not a thought-through image
we are ramshackle
a homely mess
like bric-a-brac
at a car boot

There is no sleekness to our design
no colour coordination
no concession to taste

Against all rules of fashion
and all aesthetic consideration
we are happy
at ease
daft in love

There is love at first sight

There is wonder in attraction
the dancing of light on the retina
the alignment of atoms into form and substance
the perception of science as nature

Anatomy and biology raised to aesthetics and beauty
the tautness of flesh over muscle and frame
the way fabric clings to an outline
the contours of a ribcage
the tilt of a pelvis
the enticement of hollows and shadows
poise and the grace of texture

Colours and tones that blend and sculpt the imagination
the vulnerability of a neckline
the fragrance of moisture and the lure of intoxication
the glow of touch and the genius of the blood's energy
there is miracle in personality
there is wonder in attraction
there is love at first sight
I am already yours

The house is not the same since you left

The house is not the same since you left
the cooker is angry – it blames me
The TV tries desperately to stay busy
but occasionally I catch it staring out of the window
The washing up's feeling sorry for itself again
it just sits there saying 'What's the point, what's the point?'
The curtains count the days
Nothing in the house will talk to me
I think your armchair's dead
The kettle tried to comfort me at first
but you know what its attention span's like
I've not told the plants yet
they still think you're on holiday
The bathroom misses you
I hardly see it these days
it still can't believe you didn't take it with you
The bedroom won't even look at me
since you left it keeps its eyes closed
all it wants to do is sleep, remembering better times
trying to lose itself in dreams
it seems like it's taken the easy way out
but at night I hear the pillows
weeping into the sheets

The missing page

and it made a mockery of the rest

and it became the most important of all pages

and neither of us could write a replacement

and we could never agree on its contents
            only sometimes in broad outline

and there were times when we denied it had ever existed
and times when I believed it to be several pages

and it became the perfect excuse

and the amount we attributed to it could never be
contained on
                    a single
sheet

and if only the pages had never been numbered

and

The last parents

Huddled around
the very last sun
a final handful of humans
try yet again to create
one artificial star that will survive

The parents telling that same story
of how the sky once dazzled with a million suns

How
as
one by one the lights went out
generation after generation
traced a path like a dot-to-dot
to this
the final glimmer

And how once there were as many souls
in the universe as there were these stars

And how their parents had told them
this story when they were young

And how their parents had told them
not to be afraid of the dark

A prayer for the rejected

We start from nothing and build
and you may
judge down from perfection

catalogue all that we are not
measure against legends and aeons
ignore mitigation

dismiss originality as untested
discard hand-crafted as unprofessional
destroy with a whim

discount our unborn
belittle our dreams
and despite all this

again
we start from nothing and build

Skin

More skin than I could possibly need
has been arriving at my door now for weeks
There is no return address

I've tried giving it away to friends
but they have no use for it

I've taken out ads in the local paper
I've even tried car boot sales
but there seems to be a glut in the market at the moment

I had a word with the Post Office
but there's nothing they can do

I'm running out of storage space
I can no longer get my car in the garage

I've secretly tried dumping bin bags full at night
but I swear the same skin arrives back in the morning
together with the standard delivery

In desperation I burnt several layers in the back garden
but the neighbours complained
and a man from the council called round and said
I was causing a health risk

I'm resigned to carrying as much as I can about with me now
It's all I can think to do

I can see people staring at me
pitying me
whispering behind my back
asking if I can breathe under all that skin

I could post the skin onto someone else
like a chain letter
but I wouldn't wish this on anyone

Photos with my son

Johnny is not interested in having his
photo taken

When prompted he will look at the lens
His hand is likely to move at any moment

I suspect he is not sure what is expected of him
"Smile," he says

He doesn't smile
he just says smile

echoing the words
from behind the camera

The frame of the Mona Lisa dreams

Though you have looked in my direction many times
you do not remember me
Hung on a wall on my own
you would not exalt me

I have intrinsic value

but this notoriety is not of my own making
I have seen eyes filled with wonder glance over me

Like the plain sister
I see all
but am not seen
The curious and the cynical I see
the desperate and the disappointed

Like the assassin my fame is a reflection
like the bodyguard I am expendable
I know my place at court

And in all the borrowed light shined upon me
from my vantage at the edge of the glare
occasionally I see refracted
in the tiring of a gaze
something of myself

A gentle sob
almost, yet not quite, lost

Remember me
it seems to say

Remember me
and I will remember you

Logic is not a feeling

The horizon out to sea
feels like the nearest nature gets to
a straight line

Seen from any one coast
the curve is slight

There is comfort
in the simplicity
of such a vast uninterrupted skyline

Something peaceful
in the lack of clutter

With a cloudless sky
and very little wave
the meeting of the light and royal blue
is perfection

You can be forgiven
for thinking that if you go beyond this reach
you fall

adrift without compass

Summer on Pluto

In a room with no windows
I am given a leaflet

The word incurable
is printed in bold on the first page

This is the only time I will spend in this room
This is the only time I will speak to this person

Autism is a spectrum
there are degrees

Your son is mildly severe
What does that mean?

It means he will always live at home
it means he will never have a job

never have a girlfriend
never be capable of taking care of himself

You will never have a conversation with him
ever

It means you will worry about him everyday
you will worry if he's happy

you will worry if he's lonely
you will worry what will happen to him when you die

Mildly severe
benignly savage

kindly cruel
none of this appeared on the leaflet

Abiogenesis to revelations

Twenty watts amid all this vitality

My one descendant
holds a dinosaur up to the sunset
We are engaged in an exchange of energy

Half the stars in the Milky Way
shine inside this precious three pounds

Electromagnetic radiation hitting the retina
fires the optic nerve
with the enormity of creation

The alchemy of emotion overwhelms
The ache infinite

I'm told
there are no numbers or names in nature
existence is independent of the mind

love and beauty
just icons on a computer screen

I am overawed by every single atom
Moments like this I could believe in God
Moments like this I could kiss him

The eating of a unicorn

So I'm eating this unicorn and I'm thinking
this isn't right
but you've got to eat haven't you?

So you tell yourself it's OK
everybody eats them
but you know that's not strictly true

So you look for some justification, some strand of logic
some attitude, some philosophy, however slim
but you know in your gut it still isn't right

So you think about minimising the damage
but you know you can't simply throw up and piece the whole
business back together

So you say what is done is done and you have to live with it
but you still wish you hadn't eaten the bloody thing
and wonder how you could have ever felt that hungry

So you pretend it never happened
that you know nothing about it
and besides, you thought it was just a horse made up

But now you have to dispose of what's left of the body
and in case it's discovered
you have to hide the head and the horn separately

So there you are, breaking off the head and the horn
from a half-eaten unicorn at dead of night
but

The joy of frogs

Frogs need kisses like anyone else

Not all of them want to become handsome princes
some prefer a more pond-based lifestyle

What if you turn into a handsome prince and the princess really
prefers frogs?

What if you're not that handsome a prince?
Maybe you're more handsome a frog?

Let's face it, chances are
if you can get kissed fairly regularly by a princess
and remain a frog
you've got it made

If she gives you tongues
then go for it

King Canute should have checked the tides

Taking your own chair to the beach
is a commitment
fleecy on
hood up

Better to keep your limbs moving
some might say
but sitting is a definite statement

We are not just passing through
we are making a stand
sitting firm

Day trippers we are not
nor ill prepared tourists
We are stones amongst scattered pebbles
rocks amongst shingle

Bring on your highest wave
the glory is ours
we live here
we own this weather

Cueva de las Manos

I place my left hand
on that most solid

Spread out my fingers
to form a stencil

Blow kaolin and manganese
through hollow bone
to leave a silhouette

Whether we call it art
or human nature

on every continent
something survives

vulnerable as dust

Over two thousand generations call
each with a simple statement
as urgent as blood through veins

I am here
I am here
I am here

The first spark has led to this blaze

All stories are universal
All told from a unique point of view

This is the universe
at this moment
from this perspective

Whether you want to or not
you represent life

You are what life looks like
at this instant
from this vantage
from inside the vast array

The story of life
the story of creation witnessed
from the first spark
to the disintegration of the very last cell
is one story
our story

Whether you are interested enough
to engage or not
or brave enough
to contribute further
you are already part of the narrative

At this pulse
from a collusion of all that has gone before
you are life
you are the universe

you are the story

If you should ever climb a tree

I'm not sure how much weight
my head can support

but I enjoy the familiarity
the casual lack of boundaries

Without a word
we get a sense of someone

If you should ever climb a tree
I will be your low hanging branch
I want that to be unquestioned

If my neck snaps
it was meant to be

It is the most important thing
to know

In the absence of sufficient language
I would rather seek out trees
to remind you

A gift

At 7 o'clock this morning
I bring you a mountain
I tap gently on your window
and you wake half covered in sleep

"What's that?" you ask
"It's a mountain," I grin
"I've carried it all night
I couldn't sleep so I brought it here to show you"

"What do I want with a mountain in my garden
at 7 o'clock in the morning?" you ask
not used to being woken at 7 o'clock
with a mountain in your garden

I try to joke, now feeling a little embarrassed

"It's for you, a gift"
You say you don't want a mountain
You are too tired to understand
and I struggle to explain

it's not the mountain I've brought you
it's the fact that I could bring it to you
I strain to pick it up again
and wonder what I'm going to do with it now

I feel such a fool walking home with a mountain

The questions they don't ask on the census

Hands up anyone
who is lonely
or has ever felt loneliness?

Anyone who has hidden themselves away
on New Year's Eve
rather than face that hiatus
of emptiness in public?

Anyone who has dressed up
on a Saturday night
and forced themselves out
into the melee
only to return home
having not spoken to a single soul?

Anyone who has searched faces on the pavement
for a fragment of recognition?

Anyone who has stood at the edge of a window in hope?

Anyone who has touched a photo in remembrance?

Anyone who has put a pillow behind them in the dark
against the cold?
Anyone who finds a mirror the hardest place to look
or lowers their eyes when they meet someone?

Anyone who aches without knowing what for?
Anyone afraid of being found wanting?

Staring directly at the eclipse

Your feet on my lap
as we settle for the night

A shoreline to ourselves
Sunlight on water

Nature catching the eye unexpected
Fresh air intoxicating

Getting lost in art or endeavour
Music that carries and caresses

Food presented as a gift
Being surprised by genius or kindness

Your face flush and immediate
A friendly soul at my window

Hope in all forms however tiny
The comforting mundanity of doing nothing much

The absence of pain and fear
however fleeting

A familiar arm around my shoulder
The satisfaction of something done well

Loyalty and honour embraced
Minor revelations of perception

The defiance within spirit against overwhelming odds
Valour and grace in the face of the inevitable

To spite death
and make his victory hollow

Is memory thought or emotion?

Monkey bin
is a huge monkey head on a bin

It's not a real monkey
it doesn't move or make a noise
it has no arms or legs or body
just a head on top of a waste bin

This is Johnny's favourite bit of the zoo
Mine too

Johnny did like the penguins
It's a relief to know what he likes
or doesn't like
it's probably the basis of all
personality

He hates erratic noise
dogs and babies or
young girls who can't get what they want

I was drawn to the infant giraffes
awkward and strangely poetic
Johnny wasn't impressed
the moment came and went

The tiger intimidated
I could see in his eyes
he'd fuck me up if he could

I'm sure there were other animals
real monkeys and shit

but the only animals I remember
apart from monkey bin

are the giraffes, the tiger and
the penguins
and what I felt when I saw them

It's more the feeling I recall
and a yearning
for connection

Beauty without numbers

Presented with Colour By Numbers
he chooses only what colour he wants
only what borders appeal

The figurative made abstract
The shape of the world embellished

New edges imagined
The pallet reinvigorated

A choice is braved
A universe decided
Personality shaming mathematics

Lines enhanced as never before
to create
a map of self-determination

This is not a house of war

Everything I want for my children
I want for your children

Everything I wish for me
I wish for you

This is not a house of fear
This is a house of life

How can I not see myself in you
If you look
how can you not see yourself in me

You are respected as much as I am
You are of worth in equal measure

You are family
You are us

This is not a house of intolerance
This is a house of acceptance

We are the house
You and I

This is where you belong
This is where we belong

This is your home
This is our home

The dream ticket

Man with obvious disability in maintaining relationships seeks all-consuming passion but will settle for friendship and the occasional shag. Doesn't believe relationships ever work but has been known to fake undue optimism.

Woman must be classic beauty, half saint half whore (ONO). Must be 100 per cent loyal but tolerant of bumbling indiscretion. Must have no friends that she wouldn't ditch just to spend a few extra seconds in my presence.

Must be available to lavish attention on me whenever I need pampering but have interesting things to do when I'm busy so that I can be entertained when we next meet.

Must have no friends that are male, unless they are grossly ugly. All female friends should be incredibly horny and desperate to sleep with me given the slightest chance.

Must be caring and gentle in bed but willing to be ravished, tied up and have various substances smeared over specific portions of the anatomy. Must cum very loudly every time we have sex. Must synchronise with each of my orgasms. Must groan and moan softly until the final stages then shout such comments as "I've never had it so good", "You're so big" and "God, I love you".

Must burst into tears for no reason occasionally and when challenged say "I don't want to lose you".

Must hate every one of my male friends. Find them sexually repulsive and inferior to me in every way. Must understand that my female friends are just friends and that's different.

Must always have a worse time than me at parties. Must hate parties, students, arty wankers, wanky art students, parties with wanky art students.

Must be completely naïve, innocent and optimistic but worldly wise. Must be young at heart but sensible. Must be practically a virgin but have a sophisticated knowledge of sexual technique.

Must be intelligent but not so that it makes me realise my simplistic thought processes.

Most importantly must realise that all the above is not a joke.

Please send tasteful nude photo.

Telegraph poles and ships' masts

Telegraph poles and ships' masts
are hard to tell apart
from a distance

We are sitting on a wall
by the harbour

With my golfing hat on
you can't see the onset of grey
or tell that I don't play golf

With Johnny's arm around his mum
you might not tell he's autistic
even at 17

Although the wooden Pinocchio
he holds to his face
might make you question

If you look closely telegraph poles
are connected
whereas ships' masts aren't

as ships sail away in different directions

Night fishing

You can choose to give these mountains
any name you want
at this moment they are yours

To the north
        no sign of human habitation
untamed ridges muted blue and grey
backlit with a peach haze

To the east
        a line of street lights
marks out civilisation
like a landing strip

To the south
        across the plasma screen
of the lake's surface
beacons appear on the slopes
and reflect
like the tracks of tears

To the west
        the lap of the wake
a moored yacht sways so gently
as if to lull a baby to sleep

At the heart
        in a small rowboat
a man and his son
sit and fish
in water from the ice age
silent as a distant star

We are greater than gods tonight
we are life

Sand between the toes

This is what constitutes an action shot in my world

The thinning at my crown is conveniently out of frame
The avalanche under my chin obscured

If I have a best side, this is it

According to my father-in-law's socks it's Monday
The mid-west easiness to his attire betrays no irony
other than that he's from Peterborough

Johnny shows the least interest in having his feet cleaned
He'd make a good pharaoh
nonchalant during de-sanding
ear defenders and fiddly bit of plastic now part of the ensemble

I use his red sock like a shoe-shine boy
buffing the digits

My mother-in-law relaxes leaning forward
her walking sticks hook the bench
like stabilisers

Autistic Family Robinson

Even behind a camera my wife is the centre

If she dies first
we will be buried alive in her tomb
we just don't know it yet

Tinned fruit and evaporated milk

So it was last Saturday teatime when I called in at my dad's
He was sat checking his racing results
I ambled across the room and turned off the TV

"Just a second," I said tentatively before he started to protest
"I've got something important to tell you"

I hesitated a moment, then bracing myself I came right out with it
"I love you dad"

"Don't be so bloody daft," he said

"It's not daft," I said, "I love you"

"Err... alright put kettle on then," he said

"No, you're supposed to say 'I love you too son', c'mon dad you've
seen *Dallas*"

"I've not got time for all this bloody nonsense, I'm off to the Legion,"
he said

So I'm following him down the garden and I'm saying
"Look dad, I'm in my fifties now and I think it's about time it was out
in the open
I love you"

And he's trying to *shh* me in case the neighbours hear

So I shout louder, "I don't care if the whole world hears,
I'm not ashamed of my feelings, I love you, you're my dad"
And I give him a big wet kiss on the forehead
"What do you say dad, what do you say?"

"Oh Henry," he said, "where did I go wrong?"

Photo-bombing God

A palm is four fingers
A foot is four palms
A cubit is six palms
Four cubits make a man

My son's skin is almost prepubescent perfect
sideburns suggesting maturity awaits

From the sacred to the unanchored
a sequence of genes mutate

geometry
is remapped

I'm resigned to the thinning of grey
a turning stubble hides my scars

Johnny is far cooler in his sunglasses
he wears a straw hat with the ease of a teenager

Nucleic acid replaces architectural design
twenty-three chromosome pairs roll

I've shaved my eyebrow in the middle
so as not to resemble a Neanderthal

We are a little burnt by the sun
I can't believe my face was once as small as his

The tree of life twists in a double helix
the canon of proportions spiral

I look into the camera because I know it's expected
and one of us has to

Johnny still displays no compulsion to conform
he has no interest in consequence

Two thousand two hundred hopes disorder
The Archangel's detail is without error

A pace is four cubits
A man is twenty-four palms
A man is twenty thousand five hundred proteins coding
A man is three billion pairs of chance

Gravestones at a wedding

Before God
we are outsiders on the edge

We can appear to fit in
until you look closely

My watch hangs from my wrist
My wife's dress displays birds in flight

My boy leans against the cold stone
head down

We are not really here
or we're too here

Awkward
self-conscious

Not knowing the rules
not understanding what is expected of us

Mirroring, echoing
not knowing where our edges are

Hesitant ghosts
checking our invitations

The ulterior motivator

I've looked for you
all my adult life

in the proudest of my achievements
in the embarrassment of my shortcomings

in the possibilities of every relationship
in the eye contact of every stranger

in the opening of every door
from the window of every train
on every horizon out to sea

in loud and smoke-filled rooms
over the rim of every glass

across every public gathering
down the line of every queue

in the glare of every headlight
in every face of every crowd

in the most bleak of landscapes
in the closing of every curtain

I've looked for you

A kind of loving

She came home one day and he'd gone
In his favourite chair he'd left a yoghurt
Unaccustomed to change
she lived with the yoghurt for three years
It never moved from the chair
They slept apart
She often wondered if there was someone else
It never ate what she served up
It ignored relatives
She would often have to hoover round it
Her sister-in-law told her she was barmy
to stick it out this long
But she knew that marriage was something you had to work at
She went to marriage guidance on her own
until they said they could do nothing further
if the yoghurt didn't accompany her on
the next visit
Eventually she packed her bags and left
It was a hard decision
You can't live with a yoghurt for three years
without it leaving its mark on your life
She had some fond memories though
of those early days,
and kept a photo of the yoghurt amongst her letters

An offering to the people of the mounds

I am wearing hand-me-downs from my son
at the edge of these white cliffs
where the grass is at its greenest

We are an army of one
three heads
six arms
strong in faith and valour

Our passion is unrecorded
in the book of invasions

Our small rebellion
may not be legend

but imagination is the greatest freedom
and no matter how poor
you can always afford ancestors

I wave farewell
from Niall of the Nine Hostages
from the crossbowman on the battlements
from the sons of Míl Espáine

We are here amongst the cormorants
we have reached this isle of destiny
we are the Angel of the South

Poetry is all around us and within us
This is a land of abundance
as holy as we believe

Lost amid the cloud
descendant of the High Kings

The couple next door – a sharing experience

The couple in the flat next door are always considerate enough to save their arguments until it's time for bed.

This selfless gesture ensures that their intimate secrets, their sexual inadequacies, inferiority and persecution complexes, petty jealousies, childhood traumas, parental rejections, adolescent failings, perverse lust fantasies, unfulfilled animal needs and their constant insecurity in the other's commitment to the relationship are all that much easier for us to enjoy.

The annoying thing is though that he insists on whimpering in a weak pathetic whine that's very difficult to make out. She on the other hand has perfect diction through a rising scale from full pitch screaming right up to violent hysterical frenzy, at which she is particularly entertaining. It seems a general rule for both that the logic content of the argument decreases in direct proportion to the volume and speed of delivery. Another annoying habit he has is that of speaking away from the adjoining wall and I get the feeling sometimes that he's a little embarrassed at what he's actually saying. She however grasps every opportunity to exploit this weakness and gain the upper hand by repeating his sentences word for word in the form of a very loud exclamation.

A problem they share jointly is the frequent compulsion to storm off into another room after a particularly good line. Other distractions include the unnecessarily long pauses often mistaken for a premature aborting of the conflict leaving both participants and audience alike with a frustrating sense of anti-climax, and the sporadic fits of door-banging that can so often surprise even the most careful of listeners, causing any glass not firmly held to make that embarrassing smashing sound as it drops from your ear to the foot of the wall.

Possibly the most pitifully pathetic and therefore the most interesting phase of the argument usually comes when he's ready to make up but she's not quite ready. For the next six or seven minutes he's apologetic and condescending, then after one too many rejections he suddenly blows his top stomping around and shouting such memorable classics as "I'm trying to be nice to you, you stupid prat!".

I don't think he's actually ever hit her though she's been violent, often unnervingly violent, many times, but once I understand, in desperation trying to disperse the anger, he spat full in her face. You could tell from the immediate reaction that he knew even as it happened it was the worst thing he could do. Listening to two broken people crying in the night can suddenly make you feel very lonely. At this point I usually hug my girlfriend tight and thank God that tonight the argument was next door.

The garden is still there underneath

Red trousers draw the eye
like blood on the snow
or stigmata on a holy shroud

It's hard in the wide shot
to tell who is present

We are rolling winter
My hands are stinging
my son's must be

White is the predominant colour
dark green and brown compete with black
like a stencil

Bleak but with majesty
this is our world
this is us
We are where we belong

Even in the coldest of breath
we have our own beauty
it doesn't shout
it is noise intolerant

Those footprints in the snow
they are ours

Vanguard of audacious

Kindness is bravery at its brazen best
its boldest and most ballsy

It empowers all it touches

To put your heart in the line of fire
is as heroic as it is honourable

To be gentle you offer up a vulnerable underbelly
Empathy and humanity are gifts that entail risk

No matter how everyday it may seem
to dare to act not in self-interest
is valiant

To demand dignity for others undaunted is intrepid

To find strength to confront and challenge prejudice requires courage
however uncool to cynics

To make a stand for justice, equality and even love
is never unfashionable, never untimely

To insist that tenderness endures and that mercy is victorious
you put your body above the parapet

To face injury, loss, ridicule or one of a hundred fears
but still have resolve and compassion
is a testament to an indomitable spirit

On whatever scale
the matter-of-factness of such nobility
is a quiet but magnificent defiance

Does a bad curtain call ruin a show?

I'm never any good at goodbyes

I feel too much pressure
to produce some sort of fitting climax
As though fulfilling a duty or observing the
constraints of an art form

It's the unalterable finality
I feel looming like a punchline
you know is not going to work

A polite thank you and goodnight
never seems sufficient

We expect

He'll pull something from up his sleeve you'll see
It'll end with a bang, the big finale
It's not over till the fat lady sings

He'll have held something special back
Always save the best till last
Wait for the fireworks, there's bound to be fireworks

I'm stood at the door again
having said all I've got to say, having had a great time
nervous that I could spoil it all in three seconds

Am I the only one who feels
there's too much onus on the notion of climax?
Am I lacking in stamina, character, goodwill?

Are people so fickle
that the last thing you say colours every other gesture?

Are people's memories so short they cannot cast their minds back
to five or ten minutes before the end?

I can never kiss that much more
than I kissed at the height of my passion

I can never wave that better wave
exert that extra effort
surpass everything that's gone before

So a thank you and goodnight will have to suffice

Of course
if I do happen to make a grand exit
two minutes later I have to return
having forgotten my hat

A prayer for the hesitant

A pale blue dot
amid a family portrait

This is your home planet
you are where you were born to be
breathe

The world is your living room
you are amongst friends
your ancestors, your family and
over ten thousand saints look down

Nobody means you any harm
not even God or nature
you can choose not to fear

The universe expects nothing
Every single thing is more than nothing
You have already exceeded expectation

If you forget me
my name
this moment
remember only this
you are good enough

imperfect as we are
you are good enough

II

from

TRAVELLING SECOND CLASS THROUGH HOPE

Sans pretension

We say 'cul-de-sac'
to make 'dead end' sound sunny
We say 'nouveau riche'
instead of working class with money

We call art 'avant-garde'
when we don't understand it
Jumble sales sell 'bric-à-brac'
which must be French for shit

Let's call a spud a spud
no more lies or elaborate word contortions
Chips are chips
not pommes frites or french fries
Why say 'haute cuisine' when you mean 'smaller portions'

No more saying we had a 'tête-à-tête'
when you mean you've been nagging
bragging or just chin wagging

And no more calling it a 'ménage à trois'
when you mean three people shagging

The Dinosaur War poems

65 million years BC – February 3rd – Thursday

To Hell with the lot of them, that's what I say.
This ice age is no place for a poet.
Fight and eat, eat and fight, that's all they know.
It's like talking to an amoeba.
'We need to evolve,' I told them.
'We need a thumb.'
'Warm blood,' I said. 'That's the future.'
But all they do is stomp around trying to look frightening.
Nothing much happening. Went to bed early.

65 million years BC – February 4th – Friday

'Ok let's invent fire,' I said.
No response.
'What about the wheel?'
Nothing.
We foraged around for leaves for a while.
Alan tried to charge a tree.
There was nothing we could do for him.

65 million years BC – February 5th – Saturday

A stegosaurus next to me in the mud is bleeding.
He's resting between bouts with a pterodactyl.
I explained to him about air superiority.
Suggested we improve our ground-to-air technology.
He tried to gouge me with his horn.
I've got a bad feeling we're not going to make it.

65 million years BC – February 6th – Sunday

There's fierce fighting near the ravine.
No-one seems to have noticed the ice is receding.
I don't like the look of the dust that's
blowing in from the south.
Everyone's moving out.
I showed the General my plans for an 'eco-dome'
which I believe could maintain and perpetuate a friendly
environment indefinitely.
He ate them.

65 million years BC – February 7th – Monday

This morning we came across a herd of creatures we had never
seen before. All of them were dead.
A couple of the older tyrannosaurs wanted to turn back.
Fires are burning all around us now.
It's hard to tell the difference between night and day.
I can't believe there is still fighting.
The only thing that pulls me through is I know in my heart
God is on our side.

65 million years BC – February 8th – Tuesday

I woke up sweating. No idea of the time.
I tried to find out as I have a feeling these little details
are important somehow.
Anyway the point is I'd been dreaming.
Well it was more of a nightmare really.
All I can remember was that I was dead,
and someone or something had re-assembled my bones
but had gotten it wrong.

I tried to correct them, diplomatically at first, but they assured me they knew more about it than I did.
We began to fight. That's when I woke up.
I'm not sure of the time. It was late, I know that.

Never play chess with an anarcho-nihilist

I tried to play chess with an anarcho-nihilist once
Every move I made he questioned

He continually changed the rules
but later claimed that there weren't really any in the first place

He said 'Any piece can go to any position on the board it wants
when it wants'

He kept making three or four moves at a time
Then when it suited him he moved my pieces out of the way
Sometimes into other rooms

He refused to place any of the pieces centrally in the proper squares
He declared such divisions to be 'false borders'
and started painting out the white squares at random

When I announced it was check mate and that I'd won
he just kicked the table over and
flushed my king down the loo

Ten ways to end a relationship
after Adrian Mitchell

1. *PATRIOTIC*
   I've got to dedicate myself to work of national importance

2. *SNOBBISH*
   Your time allocation has expired

3. *OVERWEENING*
   You are too fine a human to be held back by constraints

4. *PIOUS*
   I shall pray you find happiness elsewhere

5. *MELODRAMATIC*
   I'll kill myself rather than go through this torture any longer

6. *PATHETIC*
   I'm not worthy of love – I can't stand anyone to see me like this

7. *DEFENSIVE*
   I don't have to give reasons

8. *SINISTER*
   I've been sleepwalking with a bread knife lately

9. *LECHEROUS*
   I want to fuck your best friend

10. *PHILOSOPHICAL*
    Well were we really going out anyway?

All kids are born with long thin moustaches

Like most kids I suppose I was a natural surrealist
I used to think nothing of playing football for hours
in my cowboy outfit

I had no concept of relative scale
and no distinct understanding of the comparative relationship
between any two objects

My Action Man would regularly hitch lifts
straddled across a 2 inch Matchbox fire engine

Toilet rolls, shoeboxes, Elastoplast reels
coat hangers and Fairy Liquid bottles
were all stock multi-faceted components
to fit into any imaginary playworld

But never
and I always felt this to be one of the major drawbacks to my creativity
the double-sided sticky tape *Blue Peter* and *Magpie* presenters
somehow always assumed you'd have lying around
For years I pictured all middle class kids having drawers full of the stuff

Large cardboard boxes could change in seconds
from racing cars to jet planes or speed boats
just by a slight alteration in the accompanying engine noise
Any sheet or tablecloth became a tent which I'd just sit in for days
and days and days

One of my very favourite games
was when the British 8th Army desert patrol Airfix soldiers
would fight off the alien spaceship
which was always made out of Lego
and manned by Fuzzy-Felt farm animals

No game show will ever hold your worth

I noticed on your windowsill
two broken flowers in a small glass
These were not set in pride of place but lay unassuming
like children huddled in the dark

Their stems too short now to fit the vase
convenience would have them dumped in a bin liner
but something in you
could not let even this
seemingly dispensable
frail beauty die

I know such an action is no great gesture but only a tiny
moment in a far corner of the rush
but it is a victory
an everyday victory
and its colour should flutter within each heart

You, who are capable of such casual tenderness
what worlds your palms could describe
no game show will ever hold your worth
no computer ever measure your soul

whilst there is the merest glimmer of humanity
we are none of us lost

we are not lost

Mime doesn't pay

Last night I was burgled by a mime artist
He never made a sound

He could have got away with it
but then he tried to steal a piano I haven't got

He pushed and he pulled, he strained and he heaved
but it wouldn't move

Maybe, he thought, there was something valuable behind it
There wasn't

He tried to float the piano

He blew up a balloon and tied it to the piano
then he couldn't lift the balloon

I found him in the morning trapped inside an imaginary box

I called the police
He started to panic
tried climbing up a fictitious ladder

When the police arrived they let him out
He made a dash for it
tried running away on the spot.

It took the police four hours to get him into the car
he kept getting pulled back by an invisible rope

I decided not to press charges
This afternoon I put an insurance claim in for the piano

The lost generation of mermen and mermaids

I've flushed most of my descendants down the loo
unconsummated angels on clouds of tissue

I have squandered over five billion emissaries
en route to fertile ovaries

Wasted another five million destination unknown
stunting their growth much more than my own

Whole cemeteries of condoms I've created
non starters not begat but now belated

The dumped diehard deliverers of DNA
trashed tadpole triggers of the family way

Minute Duncan Goodhews that got no further
than gossamer graves and milky mass murder

Cul-de-sac germination
timely entrapment and termination

A self-induced final solution
ethnic cleansing of my own evolution

Travelling second class through Hope

With softer spine you rise and shine
and strap yourself safe in time

More beads for the natives, more gongs for the troops
you buy off the kids with spaghetti hoops
melt into the monotone, the drip-feed tv
Death Wish 4, Funland UK, until you say

Is   this   all   there   is   ?

You say you need a cause, you need to fight
you're looking for something, anything
If only you had something noble denied
sometimes you say you'd fight everything

So down at the beast market
you seek solace in your crisps
Hey, what's a nice Jaeger jumper like that
doing in a place like this?

You see Madonna singing 'Material Girl'
to earthquake victims in The Third World

You see a white car drive through Soweto
swords designed as shields
the new credit card diplomacy
and the worship of God on wheels, and you say

Is   this   all   there   is   ?

And when the party's over, and limp lettuce and lager trodden into the
carpet are no longer part of the fun. And you realise that the Earth
doesn't revolve around three pubs in the centre of town. And you realise
your God's not bigger than my God after all. Travelling second class
through Hope, you pray, there must be more than this

Plain biscuits

Why do rich people insist it's
posh to eat plain biscuits

It seems to me Rich Tea are for the miserly
and Nice are not nice at any price
Shortbread I particularly dread
I'd sooner have a Happy Face instead

Tradition is fine for old codgers
but the young at heart want Jammy Dodgers
A plain Digestive is strictly for the restive
and not suggestive of anything festive

Similarly Garibaldis
are for the oldies
as only old fogies can be force-fed
a sandwich of bogies

Morning Coffee are easy to debunk
being impossible to dunk
An Arrowroot bicky
can also be tricky

Abbey Crunch or Bourbon Creams
are not the munch of my dreams
I'd sooner walk on hot coals bare foot
than eat Fig Rolls or Ginger Nut

and I'd sooner be aborted
than touch Teatime Assorted

yet I can eat Chocolate Hobnobs
no probs

A happy ending (revised)

...and they all lived happily ever after.

Well not all. Not all the time that is.

You've got to remember the book may have taken four or five
hours to read but its story was meant to span several years.
They obviously picked out the main action and discarded the
mundane. You know, the trips to the toilet, the coming back to
close the curtains, the days when someone wasn't feeling very
clever so they just took it easy... that sort of stuff.

So when it says 'they all lived happily ever after' you have to
take it as read there'd still be days, even weeks when nothing
much happened. Someone might get a bit bored or feel a bit so
so about an idea. Someone else might feel tired all of a sudden
or feel that life was becoming repetitive, or passing them by.

The film was only an hour fifteen which meant they missed out a lot
of the book. They even spiced up a few scenes to enhance the action.

So when it says 'they all lived happily ever after'
they meant that, on the whole, given the human condition
they had a relatively happy existence
remembering that they'd got over the worst of the bad stuff
during the making of the story,
forming as it did the basis of the plot
and given that we left the main characters on a high
as is the nature of romanticised story telling leading to such
an obviously flawed generalisation.

Love like Hell

I have this theory that when you die your whole life is re-run like a sensorama video and you have to sit through it all again, every second, unedited, in a room with every friend and every relative that's been in the least bit involved. Now depending on what sort of life you've led this could be Heaven or it could be Hell. Think about it, everyone's going to see those private moments, those very private moments: farting in the bath; wiping bogies down the side of the armchair; every second of indulgent masturbation.

All the pathetic lies you told exposed for all to see; all the naff chat-up lines you used when you were a teenager, and still used later; all the places you had sex when you still lived at home. The things you did to get by; the way you justified it all to yourself and every really dumb-arsed no-balls shit-for-brains mistake you ever made you'll have to watch yourself make again.

But then

maybe

there'll be those moments of rare beauty; the moments of tenderness; the times you cried because you messed up; the things you meant to say; the questions in the mirror; the promises you made when you first held your own child; the nights you comforted another's despair; the time your lover's face glowed like beauty on fire; the times you said "I love you" and believed your love would outlive the universe. The time you first held in your stomach thinking no-one would notice, and the regret in your eyes when you feared you were getting old. When you couldn't sleep one night and lay awake sweating and praying you didn't die before doing something, something, just something.

III

from

RAINING UPWARDS

With zero the house always wins

Emptiness
is an even number
neither positive nor negative
Created in the imagination
as beautiful
a perfect circle

A hole
into which all the numbers in the universe
divide

Hard now to believe
there was a time
before quantification of that
which doesn't exist

uncontained
impossible to communicate
Only an unnamed absence

Who wasn't out to sea didn't pray to God

There is enough water here to drown every soul on Earth
We sit and watch white lines
break upon black slate

Trees and shrubs I can't name
claw at slopes whose classifications I can't pronounce

The whole facia falls bent and crumpled
like a broken roller coaster rail

These veterans
a wall-planner of existence

Humanity huddles at the inlets

Though we don't say as much
we share a cathedral sky with the distant clouds

the abandoned buildings
the quiet fisherman

the Easter sun
and the loneliness at the end of the ocean

Tunnelling into space

Why do we look for order and uniformity when
it is only though the unevenness
in the spread of hydrogen atoms
at the birth of the universe
that anything more exists

Through the patience of gravity on warps in space-time
through ultraviolet corrupting opaque clouds

through instability in generations of stars
through destruction and metamorphosis
on every scale

throuGh the random
and the chAos
the muTation and compliCation
the different
and the new

we arrive at that first connection within the womb
sparking
your
unique
brain
to life

As the ground accelerates towards you at an acute angle

If I tilt my head to the side
you are perpendicular
and the rest of this unholy mess
is at a slant
Italic trees in parallel
mark the degrees
ten past the hour

Dry leaves defy gravity
There is no slide to the east

Shadows brave the slope
The sun no longer certain
of its position

Toes grip for balance
Legs lengthen or shorten
to compensate

Fire-engine red you stand out
amid the muted woodland

You lean against the sky like Atlas
carrying all on your back

The Second Punic War is not available on a tea towel

Fortifying lungs with calm
the first sight of snow for the
elephants from Carthage pulls
at the foothills of the Alps
now folded blue grey at dusk
Closing rays reach around peaks
clutch at clouds overcoming
mountains with long memories
one shadowing the other
ever into the distance

In the room of the hospice
we talk of anything else
Barbarians at the gates
Tectonic plates colliding
Invaders so far from home

The father of tactics sleeps
eventually humbled
bled by strategy unseen
We've learnt it is hard to change
direction within the charge

The toughest hide is fragile
I can but hope a plan will
form to delude my senses
as though one could charm cancer
as though Death himself would yield

A stream of consciousness meets the ocean

Like Rommel retreating from el Alamein
we are scattered across the sand

Waves clamber to reclaim the beach
leaving the man on his lounger as a pier

Another man patrols the shoreline
wearing a watch

The wind pelts my back with tiny meteors
acupuncture en masse

I take off my shoes
feel the grains on the flat of my feet

German dad in a mismatch of stripes
washes his kid's trunks in the swell

A cowgirl and Mrs Capone
model their new hats

There's a fat man in Speedos
like an egg in an egg cup

Striped awnings that offer a sliver of cover
contort in the breeze

as though invisible punkahwallahs
have gone apoplectic

Lovers enjoying their youthful bodies
trip themselves through the water

Teenage girls adjust bikinis
Yellow buoys bob like large bathtub toys

Mums slap suncream on infants' shoulders
like basting a roast

Ice lollies drip down sticks
Kids sit in holes the shape of cars and boats

Someone's asleep
with a towel over their head

A shanty town of windbreaks and umbrellas quiver
Futile mats instantly covered with sand

Young males show their prowess and agility
with two bats and a rubber ball

A small dog bounds from group to group
scaring the nervous

There's a disembodied head in the sea laughing
Abandoned dads build castles undeterred

A group of women stand at the water's edge
discussing sea temperature and the merits of immersion

The winner of the pinkest man of the year is revealed

A youth holds a rock the size of a skull
An impromptu Hamlet

then somewhere between shot-putt and discus
he hurls it into the sea

A boy carries a surfboard bigger than himself
A head, two feet and two hands float

A family re-enact the Olympic games
Long jump is easily mimicked

Surf boy tells his dad the story of his wave
his words crashing over each other

Too late a large woman in a thong bends down to stroke the dog
This could be any beach, any month, in any year

If it wasn't for a couple with a selfie stick
and the man with the e-cigarette

Pictures of you without me

When I see pictures of you
before we met
I see the lightness
the expectation
the optimism of a world unfolding
A world before
Then somewhere between a pantomime villain and cancer
I cast my shadow on your face
I know you are still there
and you would probably deny
anything but age and experience
pulling at your shoulders

but
when I see pictures of you
before we met
I wonder what pictures of you
would look like now
If we never had

The remnants of a gymkhana

Closing my eyes in all this nature
seems a little churlish

It's the arse end of a farm
This ground is not designed for trainers

Man-made stuff sits scattered
like a junk yard

Candy-striped poles now caked in mud
lie like a kindergarten Waterloo

Traffic cones remain stubborn on sodden grass
Fallen leaves have outstayed their welcome

The rain dribs and drabs
like the last shakings of a drunk

The sky couldn't be more grey
Any British Standard colour chart would confirm

I can hear cars in the distance
Trains, helicopters even

In the field nothing moves
apart from the shimmering of poplars
forming a lofty chorus line

The gate is tinged green
like the wood is trying to re-root

This is not the rut I'm in
This is something different

Behind me a pale horse neighs
There's still hay to be had

Twigs and fences co-exist
Trees and timber
like life
living alongside the dead

"And wilt thou bend a listening ear to praises low as ours"
after Henry Kirke White

Where shadows are deeper shoulders fall
you can allow time for the aged and infirm
The hut of the old people
is given over to young bodies bolstered by rubber

Two fold-out chairs culture clash
amid abandoned clothing strewn on rocks

A flow of blood for heart and brain
excuse enough to bring your own stick to the beach

Three legs confuse the sand
Shuffle and tap lost to surf

Easing down on the front
well ordered anarchy ensues

The ten yard line ebbs and flows, fits and starts
reacts and breaks at its strongest point

We are relatively static
as the sun reflects on the outgoing tide

The world washed and scrubbed
fresh for a new adventure

All that learning and all that love
how can this not be a better day

An imaginary fly cannot be captured

After posh dessert in a paper dish
the debris of sugar scents the garden
This instant is an insect
Happiness the beat of a wing

A lazy summer evening recedes
at the pace of a picnic

Creation now sweetly attractive
our perception of time is a mismatch

Tea cups and beer glasses co-exist
as we share this flight of fancy

I appear to hold death in my hand
but mock gently as shadows stretch

You are intelligent and quick witted
Nothing will die today

in truth we both know
neither would harm the tiniest of souls

Though these human eyes are in need of focus
the joke we can see only too well

The shutter speed far too slow
timing is everything in comedy

Anticipation adds the necessary tension
It's there at your throat

Keep still, don't move
hold your breath

Twice as many hydrogen atoms as oxygen moving

I don't need to see his face to know it's him
the light has its own plans
In reality nothing is still as elements compete
A split second away there is another poem

If I want I can see a trail of silver
at the spill

or the ominous underbelly of distant concentrations
Everything I see is a reflection of this love

I can home in on the dislocation of arms
in motion

or glory in the contrast
of chemistry as liquid and gas

We may not see the same world at all
I hope yours is as full of splendour

The smell of freshly cut grass is a communication

Lying flat on my lawn
the core pulling me in
I wonder what message
the blades are releasing
This morning I have no argument
with wasps or bees
or the spiders who web
the pagoda

I half bury a stray fig
to give it a fighting chance
Even the weeds are safe
hanging on to the soil for dear life

The September sun
blesses my skin
its rays colliding with oxygen
bruising the sky blue

I try to feel the Earth spin
against the clock
Humans are not built to lie on grass
too many knobbly bits

My head needs support

Pain is telling me something

I'm already at my computer typing

This is already memory

I'd like you to know

When you feel you've handled the situation
When you've used the jargon
      applied the textbook
When you've selected only the supporting facts
      edited memory and redrawn history
When you've ignored the question
      and deftly changed the subject

When you've gone on the attack
      to avoid the obvious
      and leave no space for reply
When you think you've got away with it

When you're patting yourself on the back
      for being so clever
      I'd like you to know I can see your lies

**"And can you, then, who have such possessions
and so many of them, covet our poor tents?"** – *Caratacus*

With a narrowing of vision
the mountains could be envious of the sea
All that fluidity

Envy is usually selective
One could say it's a form of greed
or wishful thinking at best

It's not that the mountains
would want to stop being mountains
or lose their height and grandeur

They would only want to add
that extra something
they admire in the nature of water

There would be longing of course
and a feeling of inferiority perhaps
A resentment within the core

How could the mountains compete
other than with molten rock?
It would not be the same

Hiding guilt in those eyes
that avoid the waves and tides
It would never be the same

And to think once these mountains stood
so proud
the sky itself was envious

And if you
should lose your heart to the sea
how then should the mountains feel?

You've got me but who's got you?

Even the Earth moves
vulnerable in space
like an egg in a pinball machine
Lights and sounds distract our attention
from the lack of substance
like seatbelts on a fairground ride
inadequate if the ride goes off track

We hold onto each other
and force a brave face
so as not to frighten the kids

Time, rust, friction, wear and tear
and the bolt sheers

The best you can do is hope
and try to save others
Let your body break their fall

Christmas at the end of the world

It seems all old Portuguese men dress the same
as though they've come to a conclusion
At the end of the world
there is a chair so big
those that sit on it become children

The weight of the ocean
undercuts the candy-striped rocks
Termites in silhouette iPhone the sunset

In this place that others have called sacred
a light and mirrors safeguard invisible ships
waves move sideways on the lumpy horizon

The Earth spins on your finger
delicious and small
the universe is infant once more

Fame as a perpetual wedding

I've always hated shiny apple selfish people
whose lives are one big wedding
where they are the centre of attention
Their opinions
their qualities
their relationship

We bring them presents
we take their photos
we laugh at their speeches

we dress up, we wait
we clap, we cheer
we eat their stupid cake

we go home
and we give it six months

Exploring rockpools

The surface
of an alien brain
Tie-dyed green
and glassy grey

Little pools of imagination
cloudy and mysterious

Step carefully
with feet bare

Miniature Loch Ness monsters
crowd the crevices

loose stones lurk
in murky salt water

We bend to connect
and there is treasure

for certain
there is treasure

The sea encouraging
at a distance

like a parent
ready to rush in

Hominin footprints in Laetoli

Covered with earth to preserve
volcanic ash suggests that which is absent
A black and blue marble
forms the palest of lanterns

All we touch in this world
bears our signature

From a warm little pond
to the chemistry of consciousness

from bowing on all fours
we have raised our heads to the heavens

Far beyond the constellation in Hollywood concrete
there are trace fossils on the Sea of Tranquility

As we teach each new child to stand
we move ever nearer the gods

This season of new life

Nearby hawthorn bushes catch litter
blown from the beach
I pick them tidy
and carry the distraction

A thin skin of fresh green
now protects the Downs

There's a field for mothers
and their newborn

a suspicion of rabbits
at pace

At the foot of the cliff
families watch their step

The tide is at its furthest reach
There is still a bite in the air

When the sun climbs
I am able to sit for longer

Though you are always more
than a name on a bench

touching the letters

is the nearest we can get
to an arm around the shoulder

Electric like a tree praising the sky

I do a strange thing with
my head sometimes
I lift it up
raise my chin
look the world in the eye
defiant for no reason

This is who I am
this is what I am
deal with it

It's very unlike me

Raining upwards

I have shrunk with age and grief
I am not sure I have a soul left to steal
He has his mother's nose
a family resemblance in outline

Our weather-proof coats
sort of match
hooded against the torrent

Deepest blue obscures into black
on the inside
the lack of detail gives the impression
my head exists in space
like a hologram
or a dark snow globe

The mountain behind looks unreal
a photoshop composite
complete with derelict shelter

Only his hand on my shoulder
instils solidarity
and cohesion

The hailstorm has all but subsided
leaving us a little bruised
and buffeted

There will be better days
and worse
for certain

It's in the nature of ice
when the stone grows too heavy
it cannot be sustained in mid-air

I look to you
for confirmation
I am still alive

Deafness and social cohesion

I can't hear very well in restaurants
Let me clarify that
I can hear the background noise
just not the conversation
I'm supposed to be concentrating on

So people tell me jokes
and are disappointed by my lack of humour

Or proffer tough criticism
which I seem to take in my stride

Share secrets I never divulge

Ask me for things I never deliver
Questions I never answer

Make arrangements I never keep
Offer opinions I accept without argument

Horizontal amid horticulture

As I lower my head to the grass
I am shorter than the chives
Self-seeded fennel towers over me
like a monument to liberty

A cornflower weaves the trellis to gain height
Life is in competition for sunlight

The beech trees aren't big enough yet
to warrant the term trees

The poppies have lost their flowers
but not their sense of purpose

New blossom stands alongside those that wane
Passion flowers drape like curtains beside the swing

I am no threat to anything that crawls or flies
I am at a level with the salvias though not as attractive

Olive trees dominate the skyline
The sapling of a silver birch stands like an exclamation

Figs ripen at their own pace
drawing yesterday's rainfall upwards

Ornamental thistles brave it out amongst tall grasses
too regal to be mistaken as weeds

Unseen birds whisper secrets in Morse code

Faint clouds scour the sky like someone
hasn't rubbed them out properly

Wild mushrooms hide in the undergrowth
like lost golf balls

There's more to lemons than being yellow

Alone with my lad and the waves
we brave the collapse of the cliff edge
A wading fisherman is bullied by the tides
There is a mist way out at sea
but the freshness on the margin
invigorates the skin

Debris around our feet
Life trying to keep hold
Lungs expand to fill all thought

I am here and consciously alive

We've crossed the line between
existence and exaltation
as though commonplace

Whether a shrine or a mirage
the shoreline is never long enough

Are other animals afraid of their own species?

Even on tip-toes the ceiling is too tall

From a distance though the halo we breathe
is nothing more than the shedding of outermost skin

Happiness is...
a trick
played on you by your body
to encourage behaviour
beneficial to its survival

I've lived in fear all my life
Fear of change
or the lack of it

There is fear...
and there is lack-of-fear
We could call this happiness

Anger is fear
Sadness is fear
Surprise and disgust
all fear

Jealousy is fear...
When I was young I was angry at God
for not loving me as much as he did others

and if sadly he didn't exist then
I was angry at the universe for not loving me
as much as it did others

Pinning this cloud to the page
it appears to take up less space

Happiness is perhaps
an illusion of control
or an acceptance
of the lack of it

If you never saw this tree it must be difficult to imagine its glory

There is an absence of tone to my muscles
A lack of colour in my hair
We are in the Algarve off-season
across from where my wife buys gluten free

There is an absence of tree, unnoticed
Neither of us is native to this land

Unused chimneys on empty houses
are unconcerned

Even the surrounding grass is without life
the steps to the car park untrodden

Lines marking out unoccupied spaces
are unaffected

There is no wind to play with the palm leaves
now only imagined

There is nothing here to lean upon
On another day it stood taller than me by far

Now scissored cuts criss-cross the stump
there are no rings to confirm age

A lack of shade
filling the space of what once was

The March of Progress
with respect to Rupert Salinger and Richard Dawkins

Evolution is only a straight line looking back
There is no one destination
Without guarantees
we step into the unknown
in all directions

From the age of reptiles
to the age of mammals

The selfish gene is not immortal
Fidelity is seldom total on
this entangled bank

This is what is
not what ought to be

We stumble, we fall, we fail
and we learn

Under gravity
we adapt to seasons and tides
through chance as much as design

We illustrate from this juncture
only what has survived

But in the richness of human culture
we carry the lives of those that falter

As again
we step into the unknown
in all directions

At the hearth of the winter sky

I put my faith in the automatic handbrake
and walk down the slope
You can take photos now directly at the sun
and although detail is obscure
silhouettes are epic against the falling star

We walk until there is only rock and waves
Looking back across the terrain
the scale is enhanced

Later waiting for a hot chocolate competes
against the final glory of refracted light

Sanctity in coral and ash

I try to catch the eye of the waiter
to register annoyance
but relent

Auditioning for the X-men in the Wetlands

Drawn back to the lagoon
two shaved apes
neither of which speak the language
doing nothing much
not a thunderbolt in sight

This day wouldn't fill a postcard
The landscape lounges

We are happy mutants
sixty percent water
three percent orange juice

The sea and sky
an agreed grey

Elephant clouds
stepping the Pillars of Hercules
Pale amber kissing the dunes

The smile on my son's face
making the moment immortal

Windswept and drunk on oxygen

I sit with my dead brother
by the Atlantic
Two superheroes
disguised as my wife and offspring
try out their new costumes in the splash
I wrap myself in my son's coat
the zip a Rubik's cube

We know the routine
fresh orange, side plate and olives
hold down the paper place mats
from the magpie wind

The tide edges into the river
reversing the flow

This moment is my life
My life is this moment
Soon it will be dark
everything I now see will still be
only with the absence of light

If I close my eyes
you are still here

Pilgrimage for the agnostic

It is reverence that marks the moment
To make time and space
religious or not
reflection brings you closer
In the want of a better place
I come to find something tangible beyond myself
though I know
this is not where you are
and is never where you were

Only your body is buried
in this formal row

You live within me

You have always lived within me
even before
Why then
would death change that

It is I myself
who have brought you here
and it is with me
you will leave

Guadalupe and the navigator

Trying to explain Jesus
to my son I realise
there is what I believe
and what I want to believe
   These walls feel as old as hope
and my heart aches for a miracle
              or the allowance
   of the possibility of a miracle
                somewhere
      under the possibility
            of Heaven

I wipe my eyes embarrassed as
my wife returns from the gift shop
leaflet in hand

The donkey we saw in the masonry
is a bull
to signify St Luke

The angels on the ceiling
slaves stolen by the infante

I give the guide to a young English man entering

I'm not aware if he has a son

The sheet music of Microwave Background Radiation

Of course, the Big Bang was silent
as sound can't travel through a vacuum
In the afterglow
molecules formed
and vibrations rippled energy waves
light years in length

A cosmic chord
the scream of an infant birth
building into a deep rasping roar
and ending in a deafening hiss

Like a jet engine descending into tv static
The first tree falling in the forest unheard

The echo of this heavenly choir
deep below the octaves of the human ear
become bacterium on a bowling ball

At its smallest everything is sound
a universal string section
the DNA of reality

If you listen you can hear harmony
in the pulse of your blood

and the sadness of minor chords
heard by the first humans

The foghorn has long since given up

Despite sea fret
Vitamin D warms my eyelids
The immediate is sharp
but distance bleeds into haze
like I'm inside a glass paperweight

Sitting on the terrace in my shorts
my bleach-white legs
stare out the UV rays

If you join the dots
on my limbs
a picture of psoriasis forms

Another gift passed down
from father to son

There's a fox that likes
to mark out his territory
in my garden
always on walls or steps
never on grass

If I put my knees together
and spread my feet apart
the rays can work
directly on the infection

My back will have to wait its turn
My black tea has now
ceased support

There's a green tinge
to the bones of trees

A hot shower this morning
has left my pores open
to all comers

A fly is drawn to the paraffin
on my head
I am expecting to spontaneously
combust at any time

A helicopter
rails against
the bird kingdom

Two tall chimneys
interrupt my view
They are for show only
but not from this angle

The February breeze
still has bite
Everything competes
to force my hand

I've other duties
and responsibilities
on the clock

If I half turn
I can see my phone screen clearer
in squat shadow

This may be the last of the sun
for a while
If I write a poem
I can hold on a little longer

Eskimo kiss

One hand supports soft scalp
another removes all obstacles
you are safe again
surrounded by family
There is warmth in this welcome
gravity embraced
eyes lock and focus as never before
Generations whisper greeting

Biology reveals new sensations
a world immediate and infinite
Face to face with creation
you breath the same air

Tiny fingers realise a first grip
am I part of you?
are you part of me?
there are no extremities today

Skin touching skin
a most human hello
essential learning
you are connected still

The movement of shadows on the moon

Nowadays I find loading and unloading
the dishwasher a form of meditation

All news is weather
and I still wait for my real life to begin

Iridescent
It's the colour you don't see that's being absorbed

A different man stands before the ocean
skin as white as face cream

Only now this little bit of carbon
has finally forgiven God

I've learnt that the breastbone of an angel
needs to be far larger than mine

That once you're in the ground
you can't own your own grave

That blind mole-rats rub tears
over their body for defence

I am a man without a telescope
numbering the stars

My language is scraps
fallen from the grown-up's table

My regrets come so fast
they leave vapour trails

There's nothing I own
but these smudges of cloud

I have slept too long in one position

I've learnt Heaven doesn't solve
the need for meaning

it just shifts the location

Exquisite

Against caution
you choose to be generous
Whether through habit or will
you seem at ease with giving

as though kindness was natural
as though empathy inbuilt

And while reality crowds our eyes
and frustration and greed stalk unfettered

you choose to open your arms
against all rationale

as though to convert the world
one at a time

I am besotted

First prize

As you climb the podium
we applaud
there is no grand speech
We are the only witnesses
if you discount
the shrubs and the sky of course

This is for fun
but motivation is there
balance and co-ordination

You are the hero
you have overcome
you are ready to play

There are no medals big enough
no metals shiny enough
to do you justice

Two wooden boxes
on a piece of grass
make you taller

But
you are already taller
you are already taller

You won't find a box to tick on any form for this

It must have taken some time to build that wall
and there are so many walls
and there've been so many lives spent building them
We sit together
our backs to the stones
each in our own breath

No-one can see what catches our eyes
only a quiet body language
You could be any teenager

I could be any dad
neither revealing superpowers of
good or evil

Your hand hovers
unconcerned with personal space
We are not afraid to touch in passing

We have arrived at an understanding
almost unnoticed
we are on the same side of the wall

This is merely blossom, fruit will follow

Palm trees know how to bend to a hurricane
and regain their shape
Unsteady
I spot-check my senses

My body creaks like these old sun loungers
The breeze is in danger of blowing my tan clean off

No matter how they itch
you should never scratch spots

You can scrape your nail around them
to ease the temptation and fool your nerve endings

Only on the final day of a holiday
am I about to relax

On a mountain of lemon trees
I sit on a bench at the bottom of the garden

and look back to where I live
like staring at myself from inside a mirror

The sun behind my shoulder
spoons like a lover

Leakage

I have one photo of you crying
a sole tear preserved in black and white
your cheek as yet soft canvas
sunlight surrounding your understanding
There appears a question
in the window of your eye
your pupil undilated
a confusion perhaps leaking out

This interaction is in close up
the background lacking focus
your pale lips unmoved
unable to control the tide

In the fifteen years since
you have not shed saltwater
on the outside
although

occasionally I catch the same look
on that same child face
only fleeting
as though unsure of the flood

There is a ghost on the shoreline taking a selfie

You are probably the only person
in that whole ocean
swimming with their 17 year old son

The shape of the earth is shifting
Dry sand whisks around my feet

Diagonal lines in the cliff
show how once the land was at a different angle
before the world buckled and bent

There's a hazy cloud but with no edge
like a hollow fog

Thin trees on the slope lean south
A natural groyne lies like a brontosaurus on the beach

Black rocks skulk beneath the surf
volcanic sharks with unforgiving teeth

We are a line of shells at high tide
One ship is on the horizon
big enough to carry us all

Fresh air cocoons my brain
My eyes feel haunted

We eat olives and cheese before the main meal arrives

Fish heads stare at me from the side plate
They know I've put them at the corner of the table to distract the flies

The ship nears and veers away from the setting sun
a small boat in its wake

I am disguised as an old man trying to dress too young
I kiss the scars on my son's arms
and wonder what you see

There are layers of cloud moving in different directions

As the wave retreats
it catches the pebbles
like the keys of a musical box
This scree on the foreshore
becomes like a cheese grater for water
The sound almost a small round of applause

Each wet stone blinks a glint of sun
before the next surge
towards my abandoned clothes

A short walk west
there is a pregnant woman in the sea
possibly eight months swollen

Her partner and two toddlers
at her side
on an invisible cord

At this distance
they could be any nationality
speak any language

Light rolls on each undulation

In the background
a row of headlands
line up to bless the ocean

The walking wounded at Lidl

My psoriasis does not qualify
for priority parking

My wife eases her dodgy back
out of the vehicle

As eyes view us with suspicion
a blue badge authorises the windscreen

My father-in-law reveals nothing
of his need for statins

Only my mother-in-law looks the part
leaning heavily on her stick

A stroke and heart attack at the same time
qualifies her for a shorter walk to the supermarket

Earlier I saw her lift the weight from the world
Immersed in water

her limbs as free as summer
no time limitation in sight

Once inside the shop we are in public
A world of plenty is laid out before us

Fridges hum, tills bleep
muzak underscores decisions made

A little girl with no physical ailments
squeals constantly for attention
She too has her story

My son wears his ear defenders
as the two of us sit back in the car
out of the way
and wait

in the disability space

Reclaimed

My camera can't capture the breadth
of this wind-teased ocean
or the authority of volcanic mounds
that fall away far beyond the beach
180 degrees of untamed depth
180 degrees of fire made solid

Johnny pinches his mum's skin
playful in this physical domain

Small barnacles polka dot
black boulders on the beach
smoothed by abrasion

All this ground upon which I stand
is just a bigger rock rising out of the sea

I am anchored in the present by family
We whoop and shout into the high wide sky

For a full 360 degrees our world
remains beautifully autistic

A little slope of meadow outside my window

It's only mid-May but the snowball tree
is past its best
The dragonflies have left and
only the wood pigeons and a few friends
insist on being noticed

The magnolia is already saving itself
for next spring
The wind has blighted the upper leaves

With cherry blossom now long gone
the main tree stretches out for sunlight
and makes the most of its shaggy haircut

In between the red bricks of the car port
small scraps of green blotch like
felt tip on graph paper

at the bottom of the bank the grass is thicker
a scouting party of daisies appear diffident
There's a sole dandelion feigning innocence

A squat dwarf willow crouches like a country hat
My wife wants to put two cartoon eyes on it
to make it a muppet

At a discreet distance a thin tree with paler leaf
is propped by a wooden post
a few branches don't have any foliage at all

This latest addition appears healthy but almost
like life is drawing straws

Near miss

North towards the Bay of Biscay and home
I am in stasis

At high altitude
the view down from the plane
is like looking through a microscope

An alien underworld
of random lines and patches of colour

An eggshell tapped with the back of a spoon
Algae forming in furrows
Lakes like spilt ink

Scrapes of snow
where perhaps a giant has pulled his boots
across the summit

until, in peripheral vision
the coast surprises
littered with dust from broken tiles
A straight line drawn with the wrong hand

Then
arcing over the water
a wagon train of clouds head west

White flecks in the deep blue confuse
An inversion of space

Lifting my head in reflex
for an instant I see other lives
pass in the opposite direction

Despite our relative speeds
almost in slow motion
other eyes catch mine

Considering all that exists in three dimensions
and the amount of time in any one life
and given the ability to alter speed, height and direction
you would hope
collisions would never occur accidentally

I look around for reassurance
teenagers submitting to screens
parents policing infants
all oblivious to the closeness of the inevitable

The cabin staff retain their fixed smiles
There's a curtain across the front of the aisle
that's not fooling anyone
like a dishcloth trying to cover a windshield

and I wonder if each pilot saw
the surprise on the other's face

later
as we land
all my problems
become my problems
again

Hold me with certainty in this heavenly chaos

Lead me by the hand
to where pirates sleep
where air has crossed the sea
to find me

where my skin shines
and my lungs draw deep

and leave all fear and doubt
behind me

Pivot

Looking back at my new home
the grass slope tilts the bench
a little like a dentist's chair

The solar panel on the reclaimed slates
resembles a minimalist painting

There is more in the air
than you might first imagine

The baseline from the road
dulls as it bends over and round the trees

In my son's window the backs of nutcrackers
parade as triangle, the tallest in the centre

I can see my usual seat on the terrace
now high above my head like a thought bubble

I am avoiding responsibility
hoping to justify my absence

by filling the moment with
the pause untaken

the sky is blueberry ice cream

Witness

This is a tree that knows me
I played under its branches as a child
Its weathered trunk may well be heavier
but these longer limbs can still embrace

Its shadow has stretched in the late afternoon

Though all around has been relabelled progress
it has set itself in this fickle landscape and
reached an accommodation with the sky

Of course, the sun is the same sun
but it has no sense of loyalty

There is commitment with a tree

This is an old friend
that knew well
those we've lost

When I'm gone
it will still know

and it will remember
that I spoke of you

IV

from

THIS PHANTOM BREATH

One autumn noon

The aftershave balm evaporates from my face
scenting the air

I become conscious of little patches of burning skin
on my exposed arms

I have a window
between responsibilities

There is nothing I can do now
even if I wanted to

No efficiency to be gained

I can't get ahead of myself

or catch up
on anything postponed

Behind me I hear
the wind annoying a door

There is not a single cloud
as my gaze nears the sun

only a gradation of blue to white
like a really difficult jigsaw

Dear poem
this moment is ours

You lower your eyes

You lower your eyes at the mention of beauty
as though this is for others

You subtract from perfection
as though a problem of mathematics

but it is only in the difference
that the individual is perceived

It is only imperfection
that saves us

It is easy to mistake beauty for an ideal
a construct of the mind
or something to be laid on a table
and examined

but in a greater truth
beauty is merely an emotion
and in the glass at night
you understand as well as I
that emotion is love

Don't think I don't know you are already turning away
as though this doesn't apply to you

I've come to believe all beauty is love
and all life is beauty

and I am talking to you in particular

If I could
I would convince you
that you are life and this is all you need to be
that you can allow yourself this respect
that you can allow yourself imperfection

that you are love
that you are beauty

Things to do list

1. Write a things to do list ✓

2. Give each item a number ✓

3. Tick off things as they are done ✓

4. Write stuff down you've already done so you can enjoy ticking it off ✓

5. Present as a poem ✓

6. Lose interes

The clouds surrender dawn

We have secured a beachhead
no rhetoric can match

Your red coat unbloodied
a victory unsung

Simplicity as virtue
emblazoned

There is a stillness
at the centre

Little sound
but old water
in the distance

We need no parade
no unnamed tomb

Morning is finding its way

Though this is only the foreshore
even the sky kneels before us

A line in the sand

I'm not the man with the beautifully bronzed torso
I'm the fat crab that sat next to him

I am positioned, aptly enough, beside the inflatables
A green cord separates us

There's a boat to my left in the shape of a car
with a slide on the top

Beyond that there's a ten foot bright yellow bit of plastic
people refer to as a banana, although it's straight

A dad lifts the rope for his daughter to walk under
then steps over it himself

Out to sea a speedboat drags what looks like
a cheap sofa full of masochists

To my right
a family of Germans consider their options

Skin like horseradish sauce
their limbs not as loose as the locals'

Further down the flex buoys mark out
a landing strip for small propellers

A different dad lifts his skinny son
arm floats and all, over the divide

The Germans are now the orange team
ready to skim the restless blue

The man next to me
hasn't moved his perfect physique

I'm painfully aware
I once had a body I wasted

The bearded man who takes the money
wears a thin bandana

His garden chair mismatches the sand
and his bottom half is wet

Like convenient seaweed the green twine
he uses to walk the Germans to the sofa

When the inflatable hits a wave and overturns
I am envious

This will be a memory they will cherish forever
if they live

Being in love

was about giving, as I recall
brimming over with emotion

a yearning and restlessness
as though I, the most unlikely candidate in history

and only I,
had discovered something so important, so secret

so precious and rare
so fragile

it might not survive even a breath
and only I could save it

and this had to be true
and this had to be pure

and my life depended on giving this to you
and the world in your eyes stopped time

and the world in your eyes stopped time

A photo of a sandcastle is a hymn to all loss

I hate other people's poetry
I hate it when it's good
I hate it when it's not

At such times as this
I hate my own poetry
showing me up
holding me back
like a mis-chosen lover
or a delinquent child

Today, my universe is too small
it suffocates like shrinkwrap
on my tongue

I blame my tired neurones
I miss the beauty of flowing water
Even my failings are unpoetic

There is something priceless
in simply
holding your hand

No, that's not strictly true
it's in you
holding my hand

This still image
can't do justice
to feelings moving through time

Where dust makes its home

The automatic door on my garage
stops halfway

angled
as though a salute

So I have to bend like some
arthritic limbo dancer

Inside – bubble wrap and plastic sheeting
lie loose as nature intended

A workbench that has never seen work
cowers next to a kite that has flown only once

Paint pots with very little left in
display their colour with drips from the rim

Two collapsible bikes have done just that
Wellies wait for a rainy day

There's a mountain bike that has never seen a mountain
its tyres having long since sighed all available air

A Skybox seems out of place on the ground
A door leans against brickwork unhinged

A bag of compost has taken root
Half a bag of charcoal dreams of summer

Garden Jenga now just looks like assorted wood
Nearby, longer planks lie together unambiguous

There are seasoned logs for a fire
celebrating their third birthday

Assorted shapes of metal interlock
in a giant Chinese puzzle

I shelve a box of memories
with corners already chewed by mice

I'm uneasy to remain for any length of time
as though I might be mistaken for resident

A sledge waits to slip
A bucket waits to be kicked

Eventually I get the mechanism
to return the door to the perpendicular

like a guard moving from at ease
to attention

Faith in others

We are born into the hands of others

Fragile, our lives hang on the kindness of others
We are fed, clothed and sheltered by others

We are educated and protected by others
We are comforted and encouraged by others

We put our presence at the mercy of others
whenever we are under a roof others have built

or stand on a foundation others have laid
or whenever we expect others to conform

When we get ill or infirm
we are all indebted to others
more than we can possibly repay

And when we become other

others will dispose of our body
others will mourn

Still the root remains

I'm listening to a man
buzz-sawing an elm in half
as it stands without limbs

The electric wasp
hiccups as it catches
on the bark

the whine as urgent
as a pizza
delivery moped

or the drill of a dentist
who fears the anaesthetic
is wearing thin

The tone deepens
cutting hard into
the white meat of the trunk

There's one
last yelp
then

the engine noise droops
like a head
in shame

Nondescript

Everything looks different
under this damp grey wash

Surprisingly, the grass is now healthier
than at the height of summer

The privet fills its dips and hollows
with new lighter growth

A few assorted leaves
litter the borders

Overall
there's more soil on display

and a compendium of weeds
taking advantage of the slight winter sun

Small beech trees hold on tight
to copper leaves whilst nearby

stalks suspiciously akin to daffodil stems
stand ready on parade

Olives in December defy all logic
bullet-hard like frozen peas

Unripe figs remain on their tree
with its leaves crumpled like dead moths

The yucca will not yield to the calendar
despite indecent exposure to the north wind

No one has told these visitors
about local customs

Pear, plum and apple trees
all know the score

Bony fingers without gloves
they are wasting no energy above ground

At the far end of the garden
small white and yellow flowers are clinging on

Under the pergola I find the rest of the fallen leaves
Climbers hang like matted hair

The acer is almost anaemic
only ivy sits more comfortably with the season

The tall grasses appear backcombed
The bamboo a crazy hat from the eighties

It's too cold
to settle

Flying insects are noticeable
by their absence

Even crows thaw their feet
on roofs and chimneys

Snow could only warm us

Wheat field with crows

No other animal
would sit in a tin box on a hot day

I explore the outside of things
like a burglar

A descendant of van Gogh helps my child
become as gentle as horses

Across the countryside
murder calls

like a squeaky wheel
or chamois leather on glass

Black seems too solid a colour
for this subtle palette

Straight lines betray
intervention

Geometric shapes mark out
others' intent

Abandoned skeletons
lie rusted and overgrown

Given time
nature trodden underfoot

soon catches itself

What to say to visitors on Halloween

I've never seen a ghoul
a vampire
or a zombie

I have seen a young woman severed
by a car crash
A tangle of motherhood and torn metal

I have seen two honest men eaten by cancer and
a conspiracy of care

I don't need to wear a mask
or eat sweets to remember

If ever there were angels
in which to believe
I have lived amongst them

And when my minerals rejoin the food chain
will I become evil?
Will I scare?

It's a strange custom to demonise the dead

Is it just a fear of the unknown?
Is death itself trick or treat?

Here, have some sugar
being alive is excuse enough

Poetry escapes me

It's easy to mistake movement for value

Here, only the tallest of grasses shiver
The rest lie tangled like loose string

These quiet fields are neither bored nor boring
They are too wide to be contained
in a thousand words

With spectacles and a windscreen
there is an element of double glazing
to my vision

The trail of the wiper-blade arcs
a very dull rainbow
across my view

The cold light outside
blurs the edges of faint shadows

Native birds
go about their business without complaint

There's a milk crate upside down
at the edge of the paddock

Though practical
plastic amid nature
feels instinctively wrong

says the man
sitting apart from all other life
encased in metal

I still don't know who I am
only more and more who I'm not

Beyond the far trees
Friday afternoon clouds
slope home

My condition will pass
The edges of shadows will grow sharper

Given time
these birds will sing
to the same God that chilled them

Sorry if I'm obscuring your view of God

I should have committed suicide at the age of twenty-nine
but I made a wrong career choice
and went into television

Hiding in plain sight
beside cliffs like dried blood
I ask the weight of the sea for meaning

I ask the clouded radiation doing an impression of the moon

I ask the yellow dust in varying degrees of damp

I ask the lobster who can hear the ocean from his fish tank at the café

I ask the dog in the swim with his tail held high
thrusting his neck at the oncoming wave

I understand that the truth of my experience
is not currently popular

I know it's easy to forget the scale of the open ocean
Too big for my poor imagination to retain, it always surprises

I know no amount of pixels on a computer screen can capture this
I know that language is a reflection of environment

I know even as I write
this line too will be forgotten

All the poets who had ever died unloved
lay in my bed last night

I snuggled for warmth
fearing my muscles might turn to flab before morning

Today amongst sun-dried humans
I am the king of nothing. No, not even the king

The dog waits until I'm alongside before shaking off seawater
This tells me all I need to know about my standing in this story

Though we are now in shadow the sun still lights the open water

There is a change of climate within my skin
but it is of no concern

After humanity becomes dust
flowers may still bloom unrecorded

We are born naked not nude in this forgotten vale
and the breadth of my landscapes will remain mine alone

I once celebrated a small bird in autumn colours
visiting a daffodil garden off-season

and saluted black sheep in a green field
the wind sucker-punching from every direction

breathless I witnessed
mobility scooters struggling to outrun the incoming tide

and I hid amongst lost children that were just looking for
someone on Earth whose toothbrush they could share

But these were only my small moments on the escalator
whilst you were looking elsewhere

An old wedding photo in a garden rich with colour

I hold in my hand
a smile from seventy years ago

that has led to me
dragging ink across this page

Monochrome seems
out of place in sunshine

My dad would have been 94 today
My mum around 89

Rustic posts and wild roses
in the middle of a council estate
appear a little awkward
like numbers in a poem

Marigolds and picking mint
for Sunday dinner
are childhood memories in bright colour
though these words on paper are black on white

Today the thin clouds are like
someone has scratched blue slate

My wife grows lettuces and beetroot
amongst alliums and bay trees

Distance

My wife had used what was virtually a Stanley Knife
to cut tomatoes

I dropped her off at the doctor's
one digit bleeding into a tissue

A few centimetres more
and she would have lost a finger

There was no point in expecting
my autistic son to sit in the waiting room
so we walked to the seafront

At the far end
the waves continued to fall over the ledge
of volcanic strudel

Johnny stood on one leg
the other sinking into the gloop
as the Atlantic puddle looped around us

Distracted, I finally noticed
a baby dolphin had been washed up
on the shoreline
only a couple of arm lengths away

We must have missed it
thinking it a smooth grey rock
There was no movement

A passer-by in shorts prodded it
then proceeded to take photos with his iPhone
from every possible angle before retiring

The dolphin remained
nudged by the waves

I know this sounds odd but
it looked like a perfect replica of a full-size dolphin
only in miniature
the corners of its mouth still curled like a smile

A dad and his daughter surrounded the small corpse
with white stones the size of babies' skulls

Meant as a mark of respect I suppose
although this seemed to stop the sea
from reclaiming its own

Then only seconds later
two young women walking the shallows
were taken by surprise

as a swell of water thrust the carcass
against their feet

Their whole bodies flinching
as though you could catch death

Insult to the brain

a plea to Dylan Thomas at the Chelsea Hotel

Do not pour your life down the drain
Bar as altar's no place to pray
Death is an insult to the brain

Though whiskey works to dull the pain
Melancholy leads sense astray
Do not pour your life down the drain

There is no romance in this grain
Return to Caitlin at Laugharne Bay
Death is an insult to the brain

You drown convention in disdain
Two sides of a cross will have sway
Do not pour your life down the drain

Though fate drew you to board that plane
The boathouse should have bid you stay
Death is an insult to the brain

Three times a father, think again
Go home and watch your children play
Do not pour your life down the drain
Death is an insult to the brain

Jacaranda, a long way from home

I don't know the age of this tree
but the bark
resembles the death mask of Methuselah

Limbs must have been severed in the past
knots bulge like warts or cysts

Yet from this stump branches divide
until they become redefined as twigs
lightning carved in wood

and from these extremities delicate leaves pair out
slim and elegant
pale green like baby lizards

I have seen these trees in full flower
bearing such bluepurple corolla
as though designed by Dr Seuss

Recently, I have planted three saplings nearby

I don't understand the relationship of trees
to each other
but I know about loneliness

I'm hoping this year
as ever
for blossom

A '99' in the fog

Rottingdean is a less enticing name
than this esplanade deserves

even on this dank afternoon
Only two shopping days 'til Christmas

so as a family we've decided
to hide on the open beach

My white beard draws all colour
from my face

The sky's matching duvet appears backlit
with fluorescence tubes

Kipling would have peered out
at this hidden horizon

Names as with all words
are of no significance

to the lone cormorant
posing for amateur photographers

Today it's only cold enough for a hat
or hot chocolate – not both

I'm quietly content
that my phone is currently broken

My son avoids the dog shit
and the dogs themselves with equal caution

The endless cliff resembles the edge
of a giant iceberg

or an iced Christmas cake
with no ribbon

so much chalk is an incitement
to graffiti on anything grey

Walking on top of the sea wall
is all the entertainment we need

Something wicked this way comes

It's hard waiting for sustenance

distraction by jigsaw
is a useful ploy

Laying the table
never quite takes long enough
These are small dramas

My son wears his new T-shirt
from Stratford
looking like a comment
on his mum's cooking

and I
wonder if Shakespeare
would have foregone fame
if his eleven-year-old son
could have been saved

"In thy orisons be all my sins remembered"
(Hamlet, Act III, scene i)

To walk away is a dramatic act
To choose to be but ghost in your own grief
A name forgotten soon after the fact
Anonymous to universal thief

You cannot wear thin now your triumphs past
The tallest tree in winter is but limbs
Be husband here and father; these things last
Your fame was ever one of fate's cruel whims

Now you are defined in present tense
For here you're only who you choose to show
In these now lesser words your soul finds sense
These deeds today are where your virtues glow

No more old tales told of your beauteous youth
The Dark Lady waiting now death and truth

An overdue thank you to microbiotica

You are never alone with your own bacteria
enzymes and microbes and things in that area
No fear that they are but a scarier inferior
Anybody's body's best buddy by any criteria

Right off the bat, without caveat
they produce hormones
directing the storage of fat

Not only that
without yeast
at the very least
you'd be
in need of a priest
unable to feast
in short – deceased

So we're destined to invest in the guests in
our large intestine

A healthy interest in
synthesis of vitamins
they seem to be blessed in

Mates with entwined fates
dead weights – no one's suggestin'

Fermenting unused energy substrates
they break down carbohydrates
we're not digestin'

Without gut flora
in their plethora
every señorita or señora
would for certain
    be much poorer
Gone for a burton
    there's nothing surer

No ifs, no buts
these guys are no klutz
almost six hundred strains in human guts
Hell's bells in each of us dwells
ten times more bacteria than human cells

They're the kin within the skin
an adjoined twin
a win win
There's no tellin'
where we end and they begin

I'm told that days will start to get longer

There is no Christmas in my garden
only winter

No saints
dead or otherwise

Half the lawn is as cold as sarcasm
The other half marginally less so

The divide shifts as far distant fire
eases its way towards Land's End

There's not enough cloud cover to
keep any energy contained

just ancient calligraphy brushed white on pale blue
There are no angels descending

Angry air from abroad
has disturbed the garden ornaments

The attachment for the hose sits redundant
No Magi hug the horizon

I can see between the branches of trees
that spread like a map of major and minor tracks north

Behind the hedges the coast road growls
with those heading for bargains

Lagging leaves very little of me
to meet the ultraviolet

Only the soles of my boots
connect with the earth

It's not dark enough yet
to see any stars in the east

V

from

THE DEPARTMENT OF LOST WISHES

The coaster – mighty bastion of civilisation

Sponge saucer
unsung since Chaucer

Mop twixt tea and top
Cup cop to sup up slop

Not a furnishing garnish
A guardian of the varnish
ensuring tables free from tea stain tarnish

Diverter of the drip
Leak-lagging lip

O incredible
semi-porous pedestal

Overflow screen
Go-between
Close friend of Mr Sheen

Simple plot with clever stage
to blot beverage
of whatever age

Wedge against the wet
Ingester of the juicy jet

The fine line against fluid anarchy
Comfort-cushion of the panicky

Epitome of order
The great absorber
Part towel part decorative plate
Absorber the Great

Green poem

Green are the English pastures
Green – the jealousy of lovers
Green are the fruit pastels
I always offer to others

Is red the colour of passion?

Roses are red
often the dahlia
and after sex
you can include genitalia

**Columbus thought the world not in fact round
but pear-shaped**

In 1492
Columbus sailed the ocean blue
It diminishes not his bravado
he envisaged the world as an avocado

Third World War poems

To show how easy it is for a mistake to happen

Hickory Dickory Dock
the mouse ran up the clock
The clock struck one
causing a pre-emptive strike escalating
into all out nuclear attack
Hickory Dickory Dock

About weapons falling into the wrong hands

Mary had a little lamb
She also had a thermonuclear device
the Armageddon Activity Set
new from Fisher Price

Class comment

Humpty Dumpty sat on a wall
Humpty Dumpty had a great fall
All the King's horses and all the King's men
were safely tucked away in underground bunkers

About the effects of nuclear fallout

Mary Mary quite contrary
how does your garden grow?
It doesn't

In a similar vein

I had a little pear tree
and nothing would it bear

On stepping out the door all past autumns inhaled

I wish I'd never before written a poem

I wish poetry itself had never even been conceived
that I could bring you a gift
unseen before God and the angels
like the formation of the very first star
or the first new born child on Earth

but this is not to be

Yet there is beauty in the formation of all new stars
though there are a million in the universe
and isn't each child that is born as precious as the first?

So I write this poem for you
in this way
because of poems I have written before

For even if I destroyed all my past attempts at poetry
it would be like trying to unlearn a language
or trying to forget the mechanics of walking
It is futile to romanticise naïvety and deny art and evolution

My first clumsy affairs were simple couplets
juvenilia full of basic mistakes

Later efforts showed promise but lacked true inspiration
Limericks with the ambitions of a sonnet

Once or twice favourable development
was spoilt by an untimely ending or
the breakdown of the sense of rhyme
It seems there are very few poems these days that endure

What I would really like to write is an epic
an all-time classic, a magnum opus
a life's work to be left unfinished

not the first or the last poem ever written but
a poem that would inspire all future generations
a poem that would outshine the brightest of stars
adorn the heavens and
leave even God and the angels breathless

This is the poem I would write for you

Sagrada Família (The Sacred Family)

Having spent twenty years or more
building a cathedral for the poor
I wonder if Gaudí said "Damn"
when he was run over by a tram

He left behind the world's largest folly
and a decorative effect
on the wheels of the trolley

The rhapsody of the florist and the butcher

Amid new life she skips
In death his grip is strong
She gives him her tulips
He gives her his tongue

Natasia

I loved Natasia
after a fashion
and she could have loved me truly
if only after
a night of passion
I hadn't called her Julie

Earlobes

Pendulous understated decoration
ripe for perforation
Why your creation
you superfluous elongation?

Utterly dispensable
your evolution nonsensical
Natural selection
seems to have overlooked correction
of your unwarranted projection

Is your lack of function
divine injunction
God's grin
at Darwin
making the origin
of the species
akin to a load of faeces?

Oh seductive appendage
Non-productive excess baggage

Have you purpose
or are you just fleshy surplus
An etc
without raison d'être?

Erroneous or purely erogenous?
Is there an answer to your dodginess?

Heaven sent or
hellish bent
oh cherished embellishment?

I have no quibble
only a desire to nibble
as you incite the cannibal

In defence of the moustache

It's unfair to sneer at selective facial hair
though it's hard to appear unassuming
with temperance towards near nasal grooming
Still, an untended upper lip follicle
is not inherently symbolical of anything diabolical

Ok Hitler was a fascist
and also a noted tash-ist
Stalin too was without dispute a
vicious persecutor
hirsute to boot below the hooter

However, though the tash on Hitler was littler
still Adolf did rate a greater dictator
proving the fallacy of this indicator

Mussolini was also rotten
but his top lip was as smooth as a baby's bottom

Nixon was bad though he had no
more than a five o'clock shadow
ipso facto QED, not bec'us he
had a mussy

For it is writ that it is craven
to mock the partially shaven

Though I wonder if the Bible
would have so many devotees
if the disciples
had all had goatees

You can go from Ian Botham to Desperate Dan
and it's easy to spot who's not
a full-blooded fan of Victor Kiam

If Jesus returns
will he sport Elvis sideburns?

The genius of Michelangelo

When sculpting 'the perfect man'
the real insight of the job
was making David's head too big
in proportion to the size of his knob

Titian a bag

If Titian was painting today
think of the money he'd make
by picturing his nudes reclining
eating a Cadbury's Flake

A tribute to Andy Warhol's wig

Andy Warhol was no mug
of him it can be said
he pulled the rug from under the Arts
and wore it on his head

Confessions of a closet celibate

Now lust can rust 'cos I'm bored of sex
My libido's just a place where dust collects

You know the first signs of tedium are on their way
when you actually start snoring during foreplay

Then you can bemoan your hormones as really down the pan
when each orgasm seems like a predictable rhyme that takes too long
to attain
                    and doesn't quite scan

Once a drug upon which I thrived

now the insertion of protruding bits of the anatomy into the
anatomy of another to effect a momentary sensation of pleasure
together with a short period of wellbeing all seems somewhat
                    too contrived

Where once during sex
to prolong the climax
I would go through the names of all the teams in the Premier League
                    and mentally record them

now I do the same with the Championship
purely to prevent boredom

Chelsea Hotel

As a tribute to Dylan Thomas
I got pissed at the Chelsea Hotel
and though the food was delicious
as a tribute to Sid Vicious
I threw up over the doorman as well

Lincoln Memorial

In Washington doth Lincoln sit
seemingly free of starling shit
If he was sat on Manhattan
his head would get shat on
unless he kept his hat on a bit

The trainspotter of love

She was sophistication personified
an angel with hazel eyes
unmoved by my yearning
to my passion burning
            her indifference would not yield
as the train stopped
my hopes dropped
            and she got off at Macclesfield

The department of lost wishes

"£49.90," said the man with the clipboard
"A full refund, sign here."

"I don't understand," I said, "refund on what?"

"£49.90, that's the total as far as our records show," he explained. "We don't go back beyond decimalization. Wishes made before that date come under a separate department."

"I see," I muttered, still not understanding, "did you say wishes?"

He tapped his pencil impatiently. "It's all fully itemised, wishing wells, fountains, even the twenty pence you once tossed into a canal pretending it to be magical, all refundable, just sign here."

"But I had hoped some day the wishes might..." I began

He took a closer look at his clipboard and shook his head

"I wasn't really expecting," I said feeling the need for some excuse, "I was just hoping."

"£49.90," he offered

"It's not the money," I said, "I was just hoping... I was just—"

"Do you want the refund or not?" he insisted, "I've got many more people to see."

"I don't think I'll sign," I said

He made a note on his clipboard and turning to go he grumbled, "Just once I'd like to get a signature, just once."

Cardigans to the Middle East

I have a dream
of a world without armies
A world of peace
where everyone wears cardies

Attack is ONLY the best defence
for those who lack sartorial elegance
It creates an impression to lessen aggression

Hooligans with lager cans
are never dressed in cardigans
Dr Who in his TARDIS
was never invaded by Daleks in cardies

You never see a pit bull
in a nice bit of wool
Attila the Hun
never wore a cardigan

The Marquis de Sade he
never wore a cardy
John Terry wouldn't be such a hard man
if he had to play in a cardigan

Better than a sweater or a bulletproof vest
you never see a cardy in battle dress
The UN troops would make proper guardians
If they swapped their berets for light blue cardigans

This paragon of haute couture
could ensure an end to war
So strengthen your defences
with Marks and Spencer's

I have a dream on behalf of man
where the symbol of peace and love
is a white dove
in a cardigan

Waiting for loco

My love
her beauty never pales
for her I'll wait
                forever

My love
she comes by British Rail
so better late
                than never

Middle-age spread

The eternal quest is but hassle
when in the test of youth
                you cannot compete
Five minutes on a bouncy castle
and five days smelling of deep heat

Mid-Wales crisis

My heart reminisces on a faster pace
like this seaside town in winter
but time and tide wait for no man
nor does the Aberystwyth sprinter

The poem within you

Opened to the chill of the room
is the poem deep inside you

You shrug and feign dismissal
but it is as you'd hoped
it is your poem

Private and sacred
it belongs to you alone

Guarded and enshrined
it is the very heart of you

You are concerned for its progress
You are both embarrassed and proud

and in an act of defiance
in an act of pure humanity
you hold out your poem
sure that it has its place

Opened to the chill of the room
is the poem deep inside you

and for a moment the room is warmed
and in that moment you are content

and in a world of such poems
how can anyone die lonely and cold?

The last poem I ever wrote

The last poem I ever wrote I had such high hopes for

The last poem I ever wrote was to have been so powerful
it would make war obsolete and eradicate poverty
even back through time

It was to have been so cleverly constructed
it would hold the key to the very universe itself
explain reality and even reveal the nature of God

So full of life it would be strapped onto wounds
and made into tablets and ointment

The Olympic Committee would disqualify competitors
found to have read it

Laid over the face of a corpse it would bring the dead back to life

The last poem I ever wrote was published
in a low budget poetry magazine boasting a print run of 220
150 of which still remain under the editor's bed

The title escapes me but it was some pathetic pun such as *Write Now*

The last poem I ever wrote was performed
to an alternative cabaret audience at Cleethorpes
off-season
in between an alternative juggler
and a 22-piece Catalonian dance band

Coinciding with the call for last orders
it was heckled constantly by a drunk born and bred in London

who sang in a Scotch accent
and claimed to own the city of Glasgow personally

The last poem I ever wrote was entered in a poetry competition
by a lifelong enemy

The judges, having been certified dead, were suitably appointed
as their names were unknown even to each other
let alone to anyone else

My poem came 63rd out of 7 million entries
and won a year's subscription
to the *Crumpsall Poetry Appreciation Society Crochet Circle
and Glee Club Gazette*

The last poem I ever wrote was cremated along with my body
unread
The last poem I ever wrote was carried in the hearts
of those I loved

The measuring of worth

No, my heart is not in competition
It does not beat out time racing others
It's not bigger or louder than others

I would not say all hearts should be like mine
or that my heart is of significance
Its only claim – it has come to exist

It is sometimes hard to hear your own heart
I've listened well to the hearts of others
and found some comfort in their tone and pulse

Here is the most intimate of murmurs
I offer as a tiny SOS
the warmth and persistence of my lifeblood

Merely the echoes of a human heart
yet perhaps reminiscent of your own

VI

from

SWALLOWING THE ENTIRE OCEAN

Hello

I am Henry

Not the Henry that sucks up dust
Not Henry the serial queen murderer
Not Henry the splash it all over
    almost beat Muhammad Ali with one punch
Not Henry the Fourth Part One
    or Part Two
Not little Prince Harry grown up now reverting to his real name
Not Thomas the Tank Engine's work colleague
Not Henry the Navigator, Henry the droopy faced dog,
Not Adrian Henry, Lenny Henry or Thierry Henri mispronounced

I am

Henry the filler of dishwashers
Henry the reluctant shopper
Henry the surveyor of parameters
Henry the functional
Henry the spotter of patterns
Henry the dad, the husband,
    the brother, the son, the friend
Henry the retired
Henry that sucks up dust now I come to think of it
Henry the yet to be fully defined

Some people

Some people will be wondering if everything
in the show tonight will be in rhyme
and have now worked out that it won't

Some people will be wondering if everything
in the show tonight will be funny
and have now worked out that it won't

Some people will be wondering if everything
in the show tonight will be repetitive
No – it won't

Some people will be wondering
if it will be too cerebral

Some people will be wondering
what the word cerebral means

Some people have already decided
that this is not proper poetry

Some people are now feeling pretty smug
about their own poetry

Some people will be wondering
whether there's anyone in the audience
they can fantasise about having sex with
whilst pretending to listen to this 'so called' poetry

Some people will be wondering
if they should have gone to the toilet before

Some people will be wondering
if they should have gone to the toilet instead

Some people are here because
they only came with a partner or friend
and are now re-evaluating that relationship
and their opinions

Some people are here because
they don't have a partner or friend or relationships
or opinions

Some people will be wondering
if they should be insulted by that last joke

Some people are now a little uncomfortable that
I've mentioned the word joke in a poem
which is confusing

Some people will be wondering
why I didn't stop this poem 10 lines ago
when it peaked

Some people will be wondering
if I even know what they're wondering
and wonder whether they even know
what they are wondering half the time

Some people will be wondering
if I'm just wondering about myself
and my own wonderings
about other people
and don't realise those other people
have stopped laughing
and are just wondering

Some people will be wondering
if this is his only poem
or if it's his best poem
or emblematic of his poetry as a whole
or if it is not in fact a poem at all
as they originally suspected

Some people will be wondering
why he's suddenly started referring to himself
in the third person

and when it's done
some people will be wondering

should we clap?

Complication

White and pink blossom
on the same tree

its effect
like raspberry ripple

or if you count the trunk
Neapolitan gateau

I have to look closely
to be sure

trace each laden twig
back to the root

I've seen this phenomenon once before
on my small sapling at home

Mostly covered with white
flowers

on one low branch pink petals
had begun to bloom until

I snapped it off

Perhaps to simplify the aesthetic
or to unclutter my thoughts
or just to fit in

Or maybe embarrassed
that its difference would say
something
about my complication

Dry humour – a cautionary verse

Wet suits are hard to put on
tightness is part of their charm
but too tight is the one you try to don
by putting your leg through the arm

Brighton nudist beach
twinned with Vila do Bispo nudist beach

Aside from the sand
and the all-over tans
There's very little difference at all
It is less cold so
in Vila do Bispo
the scrotums are not so small

Nature versus synthetic polymers

There are three things made of plastic in my garden –
a football sitting by the swing

my mobile
and the biro nuzzling my knuckles

Four – as I notice the soles on my Doc Martens
My body comes in useful as a sun shield for my iPhone

Ants are already exploring the edges of things
Brown paper leaves curl on a plant defiantly off-season

Five – I forgot the frames of my glasses
When the breeze drops the heat bakes flesh undisguised

An aphid accelerates past my ear on a very small Vespa
Trees stand ready with knuckles like pugilists

The lemon daffodils
are so perfect they could be man-made

In another world gardeners and farmers
would be priests

A boy can clap louder than the breakers

There is no better place
and no worse place to be ill
than on holiday

I have bent my book out of shape

The warmth on my chest
penetrates the tissues

Looking out across damp crags
to the headlands beyond
smoothed with scorched grass
time becomes irrelevant

A million creatures had to live to give me this life

If I sit at the very corner
I can enjoy two beaches
with perfect vantage
like a lifeguard

Two towels underneath me
take the edge off jagged lava

Those I love are out there somewhere
It is only a matter of steps

The sea takes a run up
to try and intimidate the cliff face
in an age-old argument

It's sad to think
this page has become a barrier
between us

Angela tells me to generalise such images
to relate to more people
but I am anchored to the particular

Sometimes when she frowns
without knowing
two vertical lines
appear between her eyebrows

Though we spin at the same speed
we don't put our arms around each other
as much as I'd like

and when she takes my hand for no reason
I'm not always ready to share

A girl with a limp shuffles across the beach
leaving a distinctive trail

An aircraft carrier has parked overhead
A flotilla of tugs surround it

The sand starts to darken
one drop at a time

Our other life is
as far away as tomorrow's weather

You can inhale the dead man's fingers from the car park

My son applauds the sea
the sky and the whole shebang

He takes his time before
dipping his shoulders

His mum models
bravery and commitment

They float with feet touching
like Neptune's bookends

This high pressure is in its twelfth week
Boats have left the marina for the first time in years

I sit with Johnny's abandoned tee shirt over my head
Henry of Arabia

The Sussex stones become ball bearings
underfoot

We pop the seaweed like bubble wrap
and lick ice lollies from our wrists

A near-naked old lady cake-walks the slope
as though alcohol just reached her legs

Her dog squats in front of us and shits upwind
then wanders into the water to wash his backside

The old lady and her near-naked mum make camp

They put up a large umbrella
like a tall man
sitting on the seat directly in front at the cinema
wearing a top hat

The universe is telling us something

Once in the car a thunderstorm
pisses its full bladder

An entire ocean falling from Heaven

causing everyone to try to remember
which windows they've left open

Not unlike the Grand Old Duke of York
but without the ten thousand men

Beyond the reach of satellites
I'm standing alone
trying to communicate

Halfway up a hill
I'm hoping
the signal bends enough to compensate

Over
hedgerows impersonating a mess of wires
I notice moss on the roofs of farm houses

Fields curve away in all directions
Tractor tracks resemble waffles
I cross the cattle grid and I have bars

Through the leaves of a distant sycamore
I can see the blades of a windmill
waving

Where tarmac has become dirt
amongst nettles and ivy
I hold plastic and metal to my ear

Even
at the sound of the phone in the hall ringing
                                        I am home

I take the twenty-first century into my garden

It's already there of course

From a child's swing I see
the tall grass offers affirmation

though there's not breeze enough
to challenge the rust on the windmill

I'm unsure whether it's orange blossom
or honeysuckle that sweetens the air

Certain seagulls seem too large to fly
as if pillows with wings

The fuselage of a jet catching the sun
becomes a torpedo or missile

Chives and ornamental thistles show
nature is not ashamed to stand phallic

The hose lurks on the lawn
a snake playing dead

The olive trees have formed a hedge
Bamboo now encircles the trampoline

A lone butterfly white as a moth
tacks its way through lavender

The silver birch at the focal point
leans

like it's giving summer a high five

Paranoia

Seagulls love to shit
down my window

It takes some effort
There's nowhere to perch

so they must have to
veer in flight

and without colliding
into glass or surround

with skater-like grace
curve and curl up and away

risking damage or mortality
in order to precision bomb

Given the number of places
to excrete in the world

and the amount of off-white
on my window

there's either one
dedicated defecator

or an elaborate avian
conspiracy

Maybe guano
is evenly distributed around the globe

and I am just more conscious
when it obscures my view

The idea that a creature would migrate
thousands of miles crossing continents

specifically to irritate me
is impressive

Maybe it's gull guerrilla
street art

or maybe the birds are simply scared
by their own reflection

**Through my car windscreen in the rain
I can recreate impressionism**

Lines approximate themselves
bending round and over droplets

Shapes fudge their edges
in a universal squint

A trio of water butts
become three dabs
from a small palette knife

Planks become waves
Doors – bite marks

If I move my head to and fro
a surf rolls along the fence

The side of the shed bulges like an alien
moving under skin

Poem in the shape of an arts grant application

1a. To whomsoever sits in judgement
on the dishing out of other people's money
based on the completion of preset forms

2a. I'd like to apply for a grant
to complete next year's grant application papers
over a period of twelve months
exclusive of any further endeavour

3a. I guarantee to produce no work of benefit
to the public other than the perpetual
funding of my own application process

4a. I promise to fully monitor and record this process
and file the essential completed feedback forms throughout

4b. The documentation of my documentation
will involve the highest creative excellence
without the worry of adverse consumer reaction
or public perception
being completely inwardly focussed

5a. I would confirm I am an equal opportunity grantee
and promise to take money off any Arts Organisation
irrespective of class, creed, colour, nationality,
physical or mental ability, gender or sexual orientation

6a. It is my hope that your commitment to this ambitious project
(albeit merely financially)
will serve to help demystify the funding process
and thereby demystify the arts themselves
at the very least
to me

6b. I realise this is not an original idea
6b. (supplementary) so I believe it should present no difficulties

Diary for no-one in particular

The house is so clean and tidy
if I were to die now
it would be convenient for all concerned
apart from me, of course

I have an hour
before my next responsibility
and if I can avert death for this period
I have myself an unexpected bonus

Yes, there are things
to be done in the future
but not
for the next sixty minutes

I can sit and watch the waves
busy clambering nowhere
A bird outside my window
sounds like a new born lamb

If I lay my head down
the horizon becomes vertical
Land and sea just east and west
and I wonder which eye will close first

Abusive body language

You sit with your arms crossed
defensive like a portcullis

You could be hugging yourself
for comfort

Your hand supports your chin
the first two fingers giving me the V sign

It could be a comfortable position for you or
an intention to display curiosity or interest

Your index finger sits before your mouth
as though stopping yourself from speaking

You hang at the door
half in half out seemingly
judging each sentence
to see whether it is worth staying

teetering on each individual word

Your middle finger pushes back your glasses
pointedly giving me the bird
and I wonder if you'd display that gesture
without specs

I take off my own glasses and demonstrate

It is only when you laugh
I know I can relax

though I listen carefully
to ensure the sound is not hollow

Foreword for a book of poetry I have not actually read

We have here a collection of poems
the likes of which
I've never seen

The first poem starts us off
and from then on it's non-stop poems
as poem after poem comes at you
one after another, verse after verse,
until there is simply no more to be read

In essence
it is a grouping of symbols we call 'letters'
fashioned with some element of skill into 'words'
styled into an arrangement called lines

These lines then build into structual
entities considered 'poems'
by the author
and are then placed on pages
in numerically ascending order
to form what is regarded
or more often than not disregarded
as a 'poetry book'

With a contents page
at the front and
copyright naming this author
I can categorically state
this particular collection forms
a book
unlike any other
by this publisher

in this font
with its
unique ISBN number

Books like this need to be read
to be appreciated and understood

What I can say is that barring loss or damage
this is a collection you can
read again and again
technically

I must admit to this day
merely the sight of the cover alone
leaves me asking questions

I am more than certain
there's nothing I can honestly tell you
that can capture the experience
of actually
reading these poems
for yourself

I can hear my son enjoying colour

Rainbows hide
in white light

Burnt chicory hangs sweet in the air
There's not a blemish in this February sky

I scrunch up my shorts
to capture more sunshine on my thighs

There's no pressure to enjoy myself
so at last I can relax and enjoy myself

The thermometer never gets a minute's rest
Each breeze tests its metal

We have a tree that's not decided yet
whether it's lime or lemon

I expose my lower back to the sun
and try to gauge the optimum duration

to balance risk and benefit
My scars look better with a tan

A nearby bird machine-sews a hem
with a hundred sides

Angela sings as she slices tomatoes and onion
Japanese tea warms my throat

I am not without pain
but it is proportionate

with the age of my joints
and the decay of my sinews

I'm conscious that my bladder
seems on permanent amber

Though
today will not go down in any history books

if we were to chart happiness
this is a day to remember

Queen Victoria and her Nottingham lace stockings

Albert removed the royal lace
whilst Victoria she would sit
From the number of kids they had
he did that quite a bit

Privates' progress

En suite
replacing outside loo
From the luxury of your own silk sheets
you can hear your partner poo

A compendium of woes

Not antique
we are vintage

Pre-loved

From plum to prune
our world has shrunk inside our clothes

Where once sleep healed
new pains greet the day

Time
has become a faulty immune system

We are over-conscious of anatomy
in a conspiracy of internal landscape

Even where appearance presents the same
strength is missing

We are flimsy like painted scenery
or a chocolate egg

Tiredness leaves us intolerant to movement
and slows ambition

Activity that was once so vital
now belongs to others

Enjoy the lairiness of youth
and the smugness of middle age

If you live long enough
you will join us

one ailment at a time

Sharing a summer sunset

You might think this the still
of early evening

but assorted birds compete in song
like an overdue dawn chorus

Overhead a cornflower canvas
is brushed with watercolours

as it nears the horizon
becoming smudges of pink and white

Gulls lope from one roof to another
seemingly without reason

On the top of the trellis
a lone magpie spars with the invisible

ducking his head
as if dodging a blow

Insects too small and too quick to identify
play with my peripheral vision

A Jumbo Jet close to Heaven boasts
its bass tones

I can hear the coast road
sighing with late traffic

Different sizes and shapes of silhouette
making little or no sound

wing their way
from one point of the compass to another

The sea though low
never allows itself rest

Night calls
from ever more distant gardens

If I sit with one leg crossed over my knee
it rises and falls with my pulse

Review of the show

There was naturally
apprehension at the start
but the audience soon settled
and became worthy of this great poet

Henry's charismatic presence and assured presentation
coupled with his unequalled modesty
helped those unfamiliar with the subtle sophistication
of his poetry to relax and in some cases orgasm

Towards the latter stages
a few deluded fools
were still not convinced
by the awesome power
of Henry's lyrical invention
but even these diehard traditionalists
at the end, humbled and apologetic
had to admit
often through uncontrollable tears
and self-flagellation
that their whole concept
of what was possible in poetry
had been changed

and that they
pitiful and pathetic
as they were
cowed and shamefaced
had now been forced to reasses
not only their misguided view of creativity
but their entire hitherto wasted existence

In repentance some former critics
savagely ripped out their own tongues
and hacked off their typing fingers
leaving their writing hands
as bleeding festering stumps
which Henry insisted was unnecessary
though wholly understandable
(if a bit attention seeking)

There were calls for Henry to be
given an OBE, a Knighthood, The Freedom of Newhaven,
a Dukedom, an Earldom, a Duke of Earl-dom,
World Laureate, Emperor, Pontiff, Messiah, Greatest Human Ever,
Best Mammal and Best Known Life Form (in any category)

Poetry Please received so many requests for his work
it is to be renamed *Henry Please*

Unable to hold back
aliens finally decided
this was the right moment to make themselves visible
in order to give this 'People's Poet' the standing ovation
throughout the universe that he deserves

The sun and the moon were seen to wink at each other knowingly

The Milky Way did a high five with Andromeda

and all the gods that had ever been invented
bowed their heads in recognition

Even the Big Bang had to concede
it had been outdone

Five trillion stars, a smiley face and a thumbs up
PN Review

How are you?

How would you like me to list my ailments?

In alphabetical order?
In chronological order?
In order of annoyance?

In order of severity and possible fatal consequences?
In order of the obscurity of their medical terminology?
In order of likely risk of contagion?

In order of compatibility with your own ailments?
In order of social acceptability?
In order of ease of explanation or ease of spelling?

In order of surface area of skin or volume of body parts affected?
In order of likelihood to induce nausea?
In order of my favourites?

A rented cremation

The vicar at my brother's funeral
was a bit full of himself

seemingly on a strict time schedule
with us just another set of mourners

Punters
as you might say if this were show business

It took me a while to settle
into these temporary surroundings

sanitised, austere, but
functionally respectful
Candles with ribbons and dried flowers

My brother had been
trying to learn a new piece of guitar music
before he died

I'd downloaded it from iTunes
and here it was
something personal at last

As the melody played I pictured Dave
trying again and again to
master the chords

his fingers bent around the frets

the closing of one eye
on a bum note
as he bit into his plectrum

Then finally
playing
this time perfect

A close relationship unsung
after Wayne Holloway Smith

My dad didn't have a penis
That is to say
I never saw it

It could well have lived happily
in the vast roominess
of his grey baggy work pants

I can't ever remember seeing my dad
go into or come out of a toilet
I'm not sure he ever took a bath

He tended to wash
his face and arms
in the kitchen sink

I exist – so he must have used
some form of penis
or penis substitute at least once

I presume his penis
if it existed
died

along with his other body parts
and was cremated and now lies
in ash particles

within the garden of rest
mingling with his other
post anatomical residue

unless individual atoms
have escaped and exist today
in say the petal of a magnolia blossom
or the cherry on the top of a Bakewell tart

I'm fairly sure my dad's penis
if actual
led a fairly invisible life all round

I know that no penis of his
ever slept in their bed
or any other bed
for seven years after
my mum died

I could hear my dad
sometimes at night
using his tear ducts
to release painkillers
to help him sleep

I have a photo of my dad
perhaps
with his young penis
in his smart suit trousers
at his wedding

I can't help but wonder
as I look at that picture
what life
his penis might have
imagined it would have

I'm told
by people who know these things
that my dad died of prostate cancer

which leads me to believe
his penis probably did exist

This amalgam of disparate elements
forming this nameable entity
seemed to do its duty
as far as function goes
for almost 90 years

I hope
along the way
some fun was had

Permanent marker doesn't work on wet sand

If I were sitting on this beach alone
I would be self-conscious

but my family are displacing
sea water to waist level

so I think nothing of scribbling
amongst clothes strewn across boulders

I am not apart
I am in relation

I am not defined by onlookers but by
knowledge of function and motivation

I am part of something bigger
I am part of a shared experience

between the elements
and those I love

Quintessence

Yesterday was quite ordinary

We went through the usual wake up routine
Cornflakes, toast and peanut butter,
time on the computer, the iPad,
washed and dressed, word-search

The morning came and went without
much conscious thought
Johnny set the table for lunch
Filled three glasses with water

In the afternoon we went for a walk in the woods
Making something out of nothing
Angela used slowmo and timelapse
and we created little films for ourselves

Driving home we listened to music
Johnny set the table for dinner
Filled three glasses with water
and we all sat down together

I looked over to him, an 18 year old
with what might pass for designer stubble
Six foot four, muscular
a new haircut and suntan

and for no reason
I noticed
he was handsome
Hollywood handsome

We were eating dinner
quietly
like an ordinary family
I can't even remember what food

and there it was
a glimpse
unexpected
This was the man Johnny could have been

'Isn't Johnny handsome?' I said to Angela
wanting to include her in the moment
It was all I could do
to stop myself weeping like a fool

After
when I stacked the dishwasher alone
I broke like death

Unexpected
I hadn't glimpsed
the man Johnny could have been
The mourning was for a different loss

one known
but not understood until now
for there in this moment
was the beauty of the man he was

Out of place

"How old was he when he first learnt to paint?"
An elderly lady asked

I reached for a book to share a photograph
of Johnny drawing when he was seven

"Just tell me" the woman barked
She had no interest in the photo

"Seven" I said "but more-so the last five years"
She retired to a seat in the corner

Her husband explained they had a grandson
who was autistic

"He doesn't paint at the moment"
the granddad added

Visitors to the exhibition filed past
already anticipating the next painting

The joyful colours
lit up the dull weather

The elderly lady sat alone for some time
and avoided eye contact

Her frame hung heavy
Her mind elsewhere

Twelve raisins at the feast of St Sylvester

Others may light up the night
with gunpowder

but I have been this way
before

Forgive me
if I lower my gaze a moment

I cannot think of twelves wishes
for the world

Even for those we love
twelve is only a start

It would take more than a day
to tell these to myself

The tears alone
could fill a year

Let us wish for one thing now
and consider that enough

one small thing
and both wish for it

each with all twelve wishes
to help make sure

You decide
the wish

I confess
I may be too scared

Thank you

Thank you to all those who've seen me before
and chosen to come again
Thank you to all those who took a chance
Thank you to all those who were dragged
along by a partner
or friend and have suffered stoically
(or not so stoically)

Thank you to all those who stayed to the end
Thank you to all those who sneaked off unnoticed
(or not so unnoticed)

Thank you to all those that laughed
Thank you to all those that didn't laugh but smiled
Thank you to all those that didn't laugh nor smile
but enjoyed themselves despite that

Thank you to all those that didn't laugh nor smile
and didn't enjoy themselves despite that

Thank you to all those intending to buy a book
Thank you to all those who've not decided yet
whether they intend to buy a book

Thank you to all those thinking
you can stick your books up your arse

Thank you to those who would like their book signed
Thank you to those who'd rather not have their book signed
as it's a gift and they haven't decided who it's for yet
and anyway it will probably end up on eBay

Thank you to those who think you can stick your signature
up your arse
with your book
and your pen

Thank you to those couples who buy a book together
and then feel uneasy that both their names are written on it
as they don't think their relationship is going to last

Thank you to those who hope the other partner
gets custody of the book

Thank you to those who think this entire poem
is just a way of reminding people about the books for sale

Thank you to those who will see me again sometime

Thank you to all those
who would rather eat their own earwax

Thank you to those who will follow me or like me
on Facebook

Thank you to those I've just reminded
to unfriend me or ban me from Facebook

Thank you to those who'd like a selfie
with me after the show

Thank you to those thinking
'who'd want a selfie with him?'

Thank you to those who wish
this last poem would have ended by now

Thank you to those who will applaud enthusiastically
at the end
quite possibly because it has ended

Thank you to those who will applaud
the appropriate amount so as not to stand out

Thank you to those who've become belligerent
over the course of this poem
and won't applaud at all

Thank you to the one person who will give me a standing ovation
then look around and think better of it

Thank you to my mum and dad, and your mums and dads
without whom this communication wouldn't exist

Thank you to any possible God, the universe
and the concepts of time and space

Thank you to those in a parallel universe
where this poem has already ended

Thank you to those in a parallel universe
where this poem never ends

Thank you to whoever or whatever put us in this particular universe
where this is the last line. Thank you

VII

from

STRIKINGLY INVISIBLE

20 FAQ about tonight's event (answers)

1. Yes and No. Yes, it will be funny but No, not that funny
2. Well I consider it proper poetry, whatever that is
3. Yes, I do know what proper poetry is
4. Well if you don't laugh it's probably a serious poem
5. No, I won't be putting my hand up to let you know when it's a serious poem
6. About forty-five minutes, forty-six with laughs
7. Yes, that was a joke
8. Yes, this is the first poem
9. Yes, I believe you can have jokes in poetry and it can still be considered proper poetry, whatever that is
10. Yes, I do know what proper poetry is (see Question 3)
11. There will be books for sale – good question, thank you
12. Yes, I will be signing books if asked, again good question
13. Yes, that's enough mentioning the books for sale I agree although strictly speaking that's more of a comment than a question
14. £10.00 each
15. No, it doesn't have to rhyme to be poetry. I think we've established that
16. Yes, I will be answering real questions at the end
17. No, I've not got a poem that already answers those question
18. On balance I think there should be an element of ambiguity in poetry if that answers your question
19. Yes, £10.00 each. I did mention that earlier
20. Well, I'm hoping it's art not just entertainment so there always needs to be some risk of failure. There will be serious moments though, I'm sure as a mature rounded human being you'll find something of interest in those offerings ... but yes, there will be knob gags

Cuckmere Haven

Sun stripes
the Seven Sisters
like a barcode

The sea and sky
are sketched
with the same pen

Dandelions and buttercups
lie scattered
like coins loose on your dresser

A lighthouse serves little purpose during the day
other than to wait
though I know

somewhere on this misnamed Earth
there are always ships out at sea
still in the dark

How to make an underclass

There is a danger to setting yourself apart
applying different rules
making excuses however reasonable

Soon you start to use phrases like 'these people'
thinking of those outside your group as
punters, civilians, clients, non-combatants
and not before long 'collateral damage'

Pretty soon these 'others' lose all individuality
looked upon as worse than animals
more like insects
and no-one can empathise with a swarm

You can herd 'these people' into pens
police them differently
judge them differently

lie to them
lie about them
deny their voice
take away their rights

you can bully them with sticks
you can tax them into poverty
you can leave their dead children on beaches

but there is a danger to setting yourself apart
you are diminished
you become less than human
you become the underclass

Philosophical tapas

You can have evolution
as well as a God of Creation
It's what I like to call
A Darwin-win situation

**The only flags on the moon are white
(based on official NASA statistics)**

When peering at the moon
imagine in your view
3 abandoned cars
2 golf balls
and 96 bags of poo

Under a mackerel sky like alien skin

This strangely fluorescent
strip lighting blurs our outlines

Trunks
the colour of Opal Fruits

jar with tee-shirts and mountains
in matching stripes

Black mashed potato cliffs teased with a fork
add monochrome to the mix

Abandoned rope at our feet
is mermaid's hair

I can taste the salt
on my spit

Two fishing rods stand
like goalposts in the sand

The sea is doing its thing
My eyes brimming

Eavesdropping on the gossip of small birds

I can finally settle by the apple blossom
for the first time this spring

The ground soil remains an empty book
as yet

You can't help but breathe in jasmine
even at the far corners of the lawn

Primroses line the path
like emergency lighting

The odd tulip sparks
amongst the rosemary, sage and fennel

Dandelions and daffodils huddle
in their own little cliques

The blue roof seems to fade at the horizon
as it meets the darker lino of sea lanes

Slanting into the west
the spring sun starts to pack away

There's more work to do for sure
but that's for another spin

Sitting with Colin Orchard at Stanmer Park

The wind is sharpest in the shadows
There's enough blue to make a pair of jeans

We face a skyline of treetops
Lincoln green offset with copper beech

A man wields a bit of plastic
to help him throw his dog's ball further

Daisies decorate the grass
like icing sugar on peppermint

A boy and girl punish a plastic globe
whilst their mother carries a bag for life

Rain machines overhead roll south
to reconnect with salt

A lightweight buggy stutters over open ground
a plastic bottle tucked in with its child

Sunlight is reaching us through
a different mixture than it used to

Colin has a solid wooden bench
with a fine metal plaque

'Much loved husband
and father'

I can't think of five greater words
to mark a man

We watch the industry of nature
turn carbon dioxide into oxygen

A woman helps her husband
move his wheelchair up the slope

To fill two birds with one scone

1. Vegetarian
To make two casseroles with one aubergine

2. Optimistic
To win two lotteries with one ticket

3. Sociable
To drink two pints in one round

4. Romantic
To experience two orgasms with one erection

The devil wore Primark

Farage in flip-flops and burkini sounds fun
Trump in a sombrero soaking up the sun
Assad in a onesie knitted by his mum

Kim Jong Un sucking on a bong
wearing fairy wings, tiara and a thong

If you are a reflection of the clothes you've chosen
picture the whole of ISIS
dressed as Elsa from *Frozen*

Al-Quaeda in chunky cords, crop top, capes and crocs
Putin in a posing pouch, pom-poms and pop socks

All these fearmongers
         would fail to alarm us
if they appeared in your mind
      dressed in Peppa Pig pyjamas

Warning – deconstruction in progress

These poems may contain irony (unplanned)
archaic inversion, dodgy rhymes and
more verbosity than strictly speaking necessary

These 100 pages have been extensively whittled down from
a total of 101

There is a distinct possibility of unabated self-promotion
in all 7 poetry books by Henry Normal

You will no doubt encounter
some overwriting, some disguised repetition
and some naïve political dogma/doggerel/dogshit

Ostensibly searching for a greater truth
concerning God, the universe, nature and self
you'll find the poet overuses abstract nouns
in a desperate and misguided attempt to achieve
something resembling gravitas
or at least to achieve acceptance
of his work as existing within the realms of the poetic

You can ignore syntax and basic grammar
as the poet seems to have done so already

Punctuation has been keep to a minimum to avoid error
or disguise it

although when challenged
the poet will pass this off as idiosyncratic style
or part of a personal manifesto for social change

The line breaks are arbitrary at b

est

Consistency in shape, tone and language
– ALL TO FUCK

Often titles will seem irrelevant or showy
including quotes borrowed from greater minds
to add a vague validity by association

Some titles seem to have been written separately
perhaps some time before the poem
Some despite the poem

Some lines are a bit nothingy, like this one
Others pretentious or faux pretentious

Some lines are too clever for the poet's own good
wrapped in his Ivory Towel

Clichés can appear without sufficient re-invention
as 'par for the discourse'

There are too many similes that should be like metaphors

Some lines successfully confront the poet's inevitable decline
whilst successfully avoiding doing anything about the 'inevitable decline'

and indeed increasing the 'inevitable decline'
by him sitting around writing them instead of exercising

or possibly socialising with other human beings in any meaningful way
that might lead to an understanding of the human condition
worth committing to paper

Some lines will juxtapose weighty matters with mundane trivia
like a cheese ploughman's of thought

Some lines will simply betray
the shameless waste of time and effort on the part of the poet
and everyone else
which only serves to firm-up the poet's sacred vow
that he will, for definite, never write again

until his next collection
being forced to continue due to a lack of imagination
to find anything better or more worthwhile to occupy
his pitifully shallow existence

Some lines may well descend dangerously close to sentiment
exposing the awkward humanity hiding just beneath the paper-thin skin

There is a tendency to undercut
any genuine emotion by the use of exaggeration
or with a knob gag
or both, in the case of a very big knob gag

Some lines are too obvious
and are not needed – obviously

It may not surprise you to learn
the poet has been found to be self-critical
and inclined to introspection
with a minor disposition towards understatement

On occasion lines will be deliberately obscure
either to disguise personal failings
or to instil the appearance of creative ambiguity

endings coming out of nowhere, a little off

like a dead mouse in a toaster

MOT for a wedding anniversary

MOT
Marriage On Track
Mutual Ownership Treaty
Membership Of Team
Made Of Trust
Marvel Of Tolerance
Merger Of Two
Ministry Of Tenderness
Mate On Tap

or

MOT
Misery Owned Twice
Mad Oath Taken
Match Own Troubles
Murderer Of Time
Monogamy Only Token
Malevolent Odious Twin
Malign Other Twat
Must Order Termination

Lady with the hood

From the tusk of a dead mammoth

I can discern the earliest human face

It has no mouth but still speaks

It speaks of an individual

it speaks of fragility

it speaks of all that have come before

The artist would never know its destiny

The subject be unaware of its significance

the mammoth oblivious

This pale ivory will outlast my likeness

long outlive my voice

and may tell something of me

to you

who are yet to be born

A little slope of meadow (revisited)

Thanks to the winter rain
the edges of the grass are now straight

The once scruffy borders inked green

A metal cormorant in the gravel
does a bad impression of a scarecrow

Cherry blossom locked and loaded
awaits its trigger

The tree itself leans north to catch sunlight
beyond the shadow of nearby roofs

In a year or two we'll need to prop up the main limb
like a pensioner with a zimmer

The snowball tree in the corner
is shaped like a perfect vase

tiny leaves and matching buds
provide colour enough to dominate the space

Soon white pom-poms
will distract the eye

The bay tree near the gate is at last filling out
with dark oval leaves like exotic brooches

Its neighbour the dwarf willow still
resembles a pile of kindling

but if you lean in
life appears at its fingertips

After Joyce Kilmer

I think that I shall never see
an emoji lovely as a tree
Sad face WTF

Shady lady – Rosa Banksiae

In Tombstone Arizona
the biggest rose doth sit
with the most wondrous aroma
fed by human shit

Disclaimer

I am not you
My story is not your story

There may be elements of my story
similar to elements of yours

There may be other elements
that differ wildly

I am not
trying to represent you

I'm barely able to represent myself
most days

If you feel connected
with anything I communicate
I am heartened
that I am not alone
in this universe
as it pulls itself apart

If you don't feel connected
with anything I say at all

I hope and pray
to whatever divinity that may exist
that he
or she
is watching over us

Hot under the choleric (an intoler–rant)

I'm prone to exasperation
irritation and indignation
resentment, discontentment
and overall vexation

I'm at the age to engage rage from a blank page
straight to irate with no middle stage

You need no clairvoyance to spot my annoyance
My lack of buoyancy has a smack of flamboyancy

Wired for wrath, on the war path
fast to fury, without jury, I adore a good blood bath
Overkeen to vent my spleen, you can do the math

I've ill humour like a tumour
at the merest rumour of a minor bloomer

Any excuse for tetchy
no matter how sketchy, I can make it stretchy

I've a zestiness for testiness

I'm often aggrieved when misperceived
so a state of peeved is easily achieved
I seek pleasure in pique
at adverse critique however misconceived

If I'm cussed whilst discussed I'm decidedly nonplussed

When in high dudgeon
I'm the consummate curmudgeon
nettled, unsettled, a full-on bludgeon

I can be miffy in a jiffy, my mood sort of iffy

Not best pleased, off-kilter and cheesed off
browned off, brassed off, peed and teed off
ticked off, hacked off
easily kicked off, seldom backed off

I don't find ireful direful, I find it desireful

I'm snappy, crappy, not a happy chappie
I'm quickly fractious, prickly as a cactus

I get narky, sparky and all that malarky
snuffy, huffy, the opposite of fluffy

I get shirty, downright dirty
typing on the QWERTY

Ratty, combatty, not very diplomatty
Chippy, snippy, definitely not hippy
Short-fused, abused, not royally amused

I do a passable irascible

Cranky, crabby, crusty, scabby
touchy, scratchy, attention grabby

Grumpy, humpy, down your throat kinda jumpy

Waspish, hawkish
spicy as a sauce dish
spiky as a swordfish

Stroppy, choppy, my moods go flippy-floppy

Rancorous, cantankerous
you are hardly going to thank-er-us

My MO condensed, I'm instantly incensed
Disagreeable for the foreseeable

Looking forward to a mid-life crisis

You will betray everything you love

You will not believe this until it's too late
You will find it hard to explain

You will look on your hands as foreign
You will mistrust your body
You will count only your failures

You will run away from yourself
    to hide in romance
    to recapture and reshape your youth
    to be the successful self you should have become

You will dress in desperation
You will drown in self-pity
You will curse your creator
You will curse fate
You will curse every decision that has brought you here

You will fall in your covers frightened and broken
You will awake ashamed of your weakness
You will not be able to catch the eye of guilt
You will allow sorrow to haunt
You will seek forgiveness without a shred of justification
You will know that only forgiveness can save you

Poolside

Cliffy, Stuart Korth, 85 Carolines

These are all things Johnny calls out
when he can't contain his joy

This morning
there is nothing between me

and the sunlight
born eight minutes ago

A single jet makes a dash
across naked sky

One feathered soloist is giving it
Percy Edwards

My son counts the liquid lengths
to qualify for an ice lolly

On his back he's as noisy as
a Mississippi steam boat

He grunts like a tennis player
on each stroke

Frozen pineapple
is gold medal enough

My skin tone moves towards
these orange shorts

Cliffy, Stuart Korth, 85 Carolines

End game

Demoting a passion to a hobby
the parameters of my dreams
it seems are simply not viable

I find I am resigned
to amateur status
with wish fulfillment unreliable

Now in my sixties I finally bow to reason
I can certainly rule out playing for England

at the end of next season

Strikingly invisible

We reach out our arms to the unknown
to everyday adventures
to that ninety percent of self

to the other side of the atom
to a passing acquaintance with logic
and the lake of tears on the floor of the ocean

to experience and imagination glancing

to a seemingly irrational creator

We reach out our arms to the very next breath
to hold on tightly to each other
and to let go

of
everything
else

The escape plan

Have no doubt
I write these poems for you

These words are an oath
An incantation

Have no doubt
I will come to you
when you are most in need

I will love you
as though you are my younger self

Have no doubt
I will find you

and we will escape together